Articles from Smithsonian Magazine's Smart News

Science
at
Hand

Keiko Miyamoto

JN033984

KINSEIDO

Kinseido Publishing Co., Ltd.
3-21 Kanda Jimbo-cho, Chiyoda-ku,
Tokyo 101-0051, Japan

Copyright © 2020 by Keiko Miyamoto

*All rights reserved. No part of this publication
may be reproduced, stored in a retrieval system, or
transmitted, in any form or by any means, electronic,
mechanical, photocopying, recording or otherwise,
without the prior permission of the publisher.*

First published 2020 by Kinseido Publishing Co., Ltd.

Cover design parastyle inc.
Text design   guild

音声ファイル無料ダウンロード

http://www.kinsei-do.co.jp/download/4103

この教科書で 🎧 DL 00 の表示がある箇所の音声は、上記 URL または QR コードにて
無料でダウンロードできます。自習用音声としてご活用ください。

▶ PC からのダウンロードをお勧めします。スマートフォンなどでダウンロードされる場合は、
　ダウンロード前に「解凍アプリ」をインストールしてください。
▶ URL は、検索ボックスではなくアドレスバー (URL 表示欄) に入力してください。
▶ お使いのネットワーク環境によっては、ダウンロードできない場合があります。

🔘 CD 00 左記の表示がある箇所の音声は、教室用 CD（Class Audio CD）に収録されています。

はしがき

　本書は、スミソニアン誌ウェブサイトの Smart News から記事を選んだ英語教材です。ス
ミソニアン博物館はアメリカを代表する科学、産業、技術、芸術、自然史の大博物館（群）
ですが、Smart News でも多岐にわたるテーマが扱われています。全ての記事には裏付けが
あり、ニュースソースの新聞、雑誌の記事や論文などにリンクが張ってあることも、科学記事
としての信頼性を高めているといえるでしょう。本書では、その中から認知科学、統計学、遺
伝子工学、ロボット工学、医療、海洋生物学、化学工学など、私たちの日常に密接な関わり
を持つ興味深いニュースを 15 本選びました。リーディングがメインですが、英語力の向上に
役立つ、リスニングやディスカッションなどのアクティビティーも用意しました。

　各 Unit は日本語によるイントロダクションから始まる 6 頁で構成されています。Before
You Read では空所に適切な英語や日本語を入れる演習を通じて、その Unit に登場する重要
な単語／表現を学びます。Reading は学習に適した 400 ～ 500 語程度の長さに編集した記事
の原文です。Reading には Notes（主として語注）と Extra Note（簡単な事項説明）を付し
ました。Comprehension Questions の A は記事の内容に一致するかどうかを問う T/F 問題、
B は穴埋め問題を解きながら要約文を完成させた後、音声を聞いて答えを確認する問題になっ
ています。Read Better, Understand More! では、科学分野の記事を理解する上で役立つ文
法（数量表現、前置詞、複合形容詞、複合名詞、冠詞、接頭辞、接尾辞、物質名詞が普通名
詞になるとき ほか）について解説し、さらに理解度確認の Exercise を設けました。After You
Read の A ではその Unit のテーマに関する男女二人の会話を聞いて空所を埋めた後、会話練
習を行います。続く B では、与えられた 2 つの質問に答える形で自分の考えをまとめディスカッ
ションを行います。最後に Behind the Scenes として、各テーマの理解に役立つ情報をコラム
の形で提供しました。

　情報を正確に、明瞭に、簡潔に伝えることを使命とする科学ニュースの英語は、人によって
解釈の分かれる可能性のある文学作品の英語などよりはるかに分かりやすいともいえます。本
書をきっかけに学生の皆さんが英語を通じて科学の最先端に触れる楽しさを知り、さらに英語
力を高め、Web 上の科学記事を楽しみながら読めるようになることを願っています。

　最後に、金星堂編集部の池田恭子さんと西田碧さんには数々の貴重なご助言を頂きました
ことを心より感謝いたします。

宮本惠子

Contents

Unit 1

Flowers Sweeten Up When They Sense Bees Buzzing

観葉植物に水をあげるときに優しい言葉をかけると元気に育つ、という話を聞いたことはありませんか。音波はその名の通り波であり、振動です。耳をもたない植物でも感じることができるのかもしれません。花にはミツバチの羽音が聞こえるのかを実験で確かめたところ、驚くべき事実が明らかになりました。

Before You Read

A 日本語の意味に合うように、空所に適切な語を語群から選んで書きましょう。語群には1つ余分なものがあります。

1. 聴覚情報は耳をもつ生物だけのものである
   (　　　　　　　) information is reserved for living things with ears
2. 花粉媒介者が近づくのを感じると、花は蜜を甘くする
   flowers sweeten up their (　　　　　　　) when they sense a pollinator approaching
3. 音はありとあらゆるところに存在する　　sound is (　　　　　　)
4. そのチームはマツヨイグサを5種類の音にさらした
   the team (　　　　　　) the beach evening primrose to five types of sound
5. 室内で生育する植物を用いて実験を繰り返した
   the experiment was repeated with plants (　　　　　　) indoors

grown	pitch	ubiquitous	exposed	auditory	nectar

B 下線部の英語の意味として適切な日本語を空所に書きましょう。

1. sound is <u>propagated</u> as a wave　　音は波として (　　　　　　)
2. <u>detect</u> the presence of sound　　音の存在を (　　　　　　)
3. the ability to perceive <u>vibrations</u>　　(　　　　　　) を知覚する能力
4. we have to <u>take into account</u>
   私たちは (　　　　　　) しなくてはならない
5. they are living <u>entities</u>　　彼らは生きている (　　　　　　) である

Reading

CD1-02 ~ CD1-09

Notes

1 It's a common assumption that auditory information is reserved for living things with ears and that creatures without cochlea—namely plants—don't tune into a bee buzzing or the wind whistling. But a new study suggests
5 the plants are listening, and some flowers even sweeten up their nectar when they sense a pollinator approaching.

2 Sound is ubiquitous; plenty of species have harnessed the power of sound to their evolutionary advantage in some way or another—a wolf howls and rabbits run, a deer hears
10 a thunder strike in the distance and seeks shelter, and birds sing to attract their mates. Plants have withstood the test of time, so logically, they must react to such a crucial sensory tool as well, right? This question is essentially the basis of Tel Aviv University evolutionary theoretician Li-
15 lach Hadany's interest in pursuing the new study, reports Michelle Z. Donahue at *National Geographic*.

3 Since sound is propagated as a wave, it doesn't always take the complex set of ear bones and hair cells found in mammal ears to detect the presence of sound. All that is
20 needed is the ability to perceive vibrations.

4 To test the idea, Hadany and her team looked at the relationship between bees and flowers. The team exposed the beach evening primrose, *Oenothera drummondii*, to five types of sound: silence, the buzz of a bee from four inches
25 away, and low, intermediate and high pitched sounds produced by a computer, Donahue writes. They then measured the amount of nectar that the flowers produced after being exposed to the sound.

5 Blossoms exposed to silence as well as high-frequency
30 and intermediate-frequency waves produced the baseline amount of sugar expected in their nectar. However, the blooms exposed to the bee's buzz and low-frequency sounds bumped their sugar content up from 12 to 20 percent within

cochlea （内耳の）蝸牛殻

buzz
（ハチなどが）ブンブンと音を立てる

pollinator 授粉媒介者

harness 利用する

howl 遠吠えする

withstand the test of time
時の試練に耐える［耐えて残る］

sensory 知覚の

Tel Aviv University
テルアビブ大学
evolutionary theoretician
進化理論家
National Geographic
ナショナル・ジオグラフィック誌

beach evening primrose
マツヨイグサの一種
Oenothera drummondii
上記の学名

high-frequency 高周波の

baseline 基準値

bump ~ up ～を増やす

8

three minutes of being exposed to the hum. In other words,
35 when they "heard" a bee approaching, they sweetened their
nectar.

6 "We were quite surprised when we found out that it actually worked," Hadany tells Donahue. "But after repeating
it in other situations, in different seasons, and with plants
40 grown both indoors and outdoors, we feel very confident in
the result."

7 Hadany calls the science of plant interaction with
sound "phytoacoustics" and says there's still a lot left to
learn about how plants perceive sound and the mechanism
45 of those relationships.

8 "We have to take into account that flowers have
evolved with pollinators for a very long time," Hadany tells
Donahue. "They are living entities, and they, too, need to
survive in the world. It's important for them to be able to
50 sense their environment—especially if they cannot go any-
where."

Comprehension Questions

A 記事の内容に一致するものには T（True）、一致しないものには F（False）を空所に書き入れましょう。

1. It's generally thought that plants cannot hear any sound. （　　　）
2. For most of animals, auditory information is not crucial for their survival.

   （　　　）
3. Although sound travels as a wave, just the ability to perceive vibrations is not enough to detect the presence of sound. （　　　）
4. "Phytoacoustics" is a term suggested by Prof. Hadany, which means the science of plant interaction with sound. （　　　）
5. Prof. Hadany started this study based on an idea that flowers must detect sound since they need to sense their environment. （　　　）

B 以下は記事の要約です。適切な語を空所に書き入れ、音声を聞いて答えを確認しましょう。　　　🎧 DL 02　　🔘 CD1-10

Sound is (1. u　　　　　　) and plays a very important role in the (2. s　　　　　　) of living things. So, a researcher at Tel Aviv University thought that plants having withstood the test of time must (3. r　　　　　　) to it. Since sound is (4. p　　　　　　) as a wave, if plants have the ability to perceive (5. v　　　　　　), they can (6. d　　　　　　) the presence of sound. The researchers (7. e　　　　　　) the beach evening primrose to five types of sound: silence, the (8. b　　　　　　) of a bee, and low, (9. i　　　　　　) and high pitched sounds produced by a computer. Then they measured the amount of (10. s　　　　　　) contained in the (11. n　　　　　　). They found out that the blooms exposed to the bee's buzz and low-frequency sounds increased their sugar (12. c　　　　　　) within three minutes of being exposed to the hum. That means the flowers sweetened their nectar when they "heard" a bee approaching.

Read Better, Understand More!

関係代名詞・接続詞 that の省略

あってもなくてもよい単語は省略されるのが科学英語。同じ内容を表現できるのであれば、言葉の数は少ないほどよいのです。本文の７段落目の文章を見てみましょう。

Hadany calls the science of plant interaction with sound "phytoacoustics" and says (that) there's still a lot (that is) left to learn about how plants perceive sound and the mechanism of those relationships.

ここでは says の後の接続詞 that と there's still a lot の後の関係代名詞と動詞 that is がそれぞれ省略されています。このように省略しても影響がない（意味があいまいにならない）場合、接続詞 that や関係代名詞を省略することで文章が引き締まります。

Exercise 次の文中で省略されている接続詞や関係代名詞を補いましょう。

1. But a new study suggests the plants are listening, and some flowers even sweeten up their nectar when they sense a pollinator approaching.

2. The team exposed the beach evening primrose, *Oenothera drummondii*, to five types of sound: silence, the buzz of a bee from four inches away, and low, intermediate and high pitched sounds produced by a computer, Donahue writes.

3. Blossoms exposed to silence as well as high-frequency and intermediate-frequency waves produced the baseline amount of sugar expected in their nectar. However, the blooms exposed to the bee's buzz and low-frequency sounds bumped their sugar content up from 12 to 20 percent within three minutes of being exposed to the hum.

After You Read

A 会話を聞き、空所を埋めましょう。その後、会話をペアで練習しましょう。

🎧 DL 03　◎ CD1-11

Evan: Julia, don't you think these foliage plants* are getting old and look miserable?

Julia: Well, they are certainly old but I still love them. And, 1. _____
_____, Evan. They are listening to us.

Evan: Are you kidding? They are plants. They don't have ears.

Julia: You are wrong if you think auditory information is 2. _____
_____. As sound is a vibration, you don't necessarily
3. _____. Researchers are now
studying the relationship between plants and sound — sound emission and
sound detection in plants. And 4. _____
_____ is called phytoacoustics.

Evan: Hmm, that's new to me. There may be other things that many people make
wrong assumptions about. Let's say plants 5. _____
_____!

*foliage plant：観葉植物

B あなた自身の意見を考え、クラスメートと話し合いましょう。

1. Do you agree or disagree with the assumption that auditory information is reserved for living things with ears?

2. Is there any other common assumption which might be wrong?

Behind the Scenes　植物の持つ知られざる力

歩いて逃げることのできない植物には動物に食べられないためのさまざまな防御方法が
備わっています。例えば、2017年7月にオンラインジャーナル *Nature Ecology & Evolution* に発表された研究によれば、イモムシに葉を食べられそうになったトマトは自分
の味を悪くする物質を発して身を守り、イモムシを共食いに走らせることが分かりまし
た。葉っぱがまずくなると、イモムシは仲間を食べるほうがましだと思うのです。また
カタツムリの粘液を地面にたらしたところ、実際にはカタツムリはいないのにも関わら
ず、近くに生えていたトマトは草食動物を遠ざける作用のあるリポキシゲナーゼという
酵素をたくさん作り出したという報告もあります。一体トマトはどのようにカタツムリ
の粘液を感知したのでしょうか。トマトには嗅覚もあるのでしょうか。

Unit 2

Sorry, the Mona Lisa Is Not Looking at You

「モナリザ効果」とよばれる現象をご存知ですか。レオナルド・ダ・ヴィンチのあの有名な絵画「モナリザ」を見る人は、部屋のどこに立っていても、常に彼女から見つめられているように感じるというものです。ところが、ドイツの研究者が実際に調べてみたところ、モナリザが見つめているのはあなたではなかったのです。

Before You Read

A 日本語の意味に合うように、空所に適切な語を語群から選んで書きましょう。語群には１つ余分なものがあります。

1. 美術愛好家がその部屋のどこをあちこち歩き回ろうとも
   no (　　　　　　) where art-lovers move around the room
2. 少なくともモナリザに関しては
   at least when it (　　　　　　) to the Mona Lisa
3. コンピューターの画面にこの絵の画像を表示する
   put an image of the painting (　　　　　　) on a computer screen
4. 人々は見られているように感じる
   people feel like they're being looked (　　　　　)
5. さらに大きな疑問が生まれる　　it (　　　　　) an even bigger question

at　　matter　　comes　　with　　up　　raises

B 下線部の英語の意味として適切な日本語を空所に書きましょう。

1. take a close look at the painting　　その絵を（　　　　　　　　　）
2. the DaVinci masterpiece　　　　　　ダ・ヴィンチの（　　　　　　　）
3. the image was cropped　　　　　　　画像は（　　　　　　　　）
4. the painting was looking to the right
   その絵は（　　　　　　　）を見ていた
5. glance over your shoulder　　　（　　　　　　　　　　）視線を投げかける

13

Reading

Notes

1 There are lots of myths and legends about the Mona Lisa—that it's actually a self-portrait of DaVinci, that it includes hidden references to ancient literary works, that there are hidden codes made of numbers and letters hidden in her eyes. One of the most persistent ideas, though, is the Mona Lisa effect—the notion that no matter where art-lovers move around the room, the eyes of Lady Giocondo look directly at them.

2 German researchers recently put the Mona Lisa effect to the test, asking participants to take a close look at the painting. What they found is that the legendary effect isn't real, at least when it comes to the Mona Lisa.

3 Emily Dixon at *CNN* reports that cognitive scientists from Bielefeld University recruited 24 participants to give the DaVinci masterpiece a cold, hard look. They put an image of the painting up on a computer screen 26 inches away from viewers, then asked participants to use a long carpenter's ruler to indicate where the painting's eyes were directed. The measurements were repeated as the image was cropped and zoomed in 15 different ways, including images just showing the Mona Lisa's eyes. The image was also slightly moved left and right to keep participants on their toes. In total, the team collected 2,000 measurements of the painting's perceived gaze.

4 The result? Most of the Mona watchers determined the painting was looking to the right at an average angle of 15.4 degrees, akin to having someone trying to look over your shoulder. "There is no doubt about the existence of the Mona Lisa effect—it just does not occur with Mona Lisa herself," the researchers write in the journal *i-Perception*.

5 Even if DaVinci's masterpiece doesn't exhibit its namesake effect, other artworks do. "People can feel like they're being looked at from both photographs and paintings—if

myth 神話

DaVinci
レオナルド・ダ・ヴィンチ

Lady Giocondo
リザ・デル・ジョコンド。モナ・リザのモデルだと言われている。

put ~ to the test
～を実験［試験］する

CNN
Cable News Networkの略。米国のケーブルテレビおよび衛星テレビ向けのニュースチャンネル。
cognitive scientist
認知科学者
Bielefeld University
ビーレフェルト大学

keep *someone* on their toes
（人）の緊張を保つ

akin to ~ ～と類似で

i-Perception
視覚と知覚の心理を専門とする学術論文誌
namesake
同名の物、ちなんで名づけられた物

the person portrayed looks straight ahead out of the image, that is, at a gaze angle of 0 degrees," co-author Gernot Horstmann says in a press release. "With a slightly sideward glance, you may still feel as if you were being looked at. This was perceived as if the portrayed person were looking at your ear, and corresponds to about 5 degrees from a normal viewing distance. But as the angle increases, you would not have the impression of being looked at."

| 6   So if the Mona Lisa is glancing over your shoulder, it raises an even bigger question—who is standing right behind you, and why is she so happy to see them?

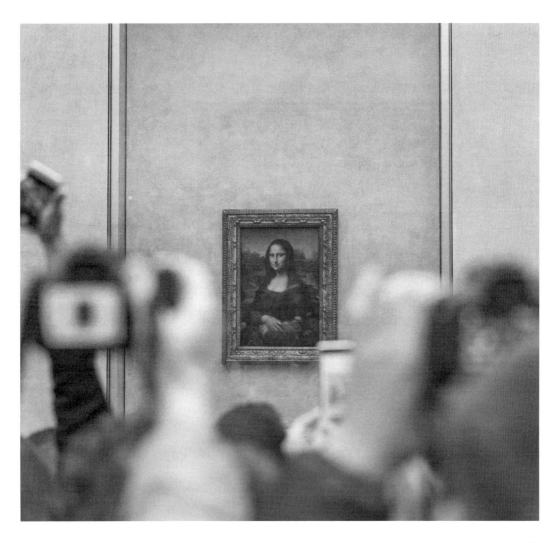

Comprehension Questions

A 記事の内容に一致するものには T（True）、一致しないものには F（False）を空所に書き入れましょう。

1. According to the recent study carried out by German researchers, it was found that the Mona Lisa effect does not exist at all.　　　　　　　　　（　　）

2. The researchers used a computer screen and variously edited images of the painting, and asked participants to use a long carpenter's ruler to indicate where the painting's eyes were directed.　　　　　　　　　（　　）

3. Most of the viewers answered that the painting was looking to the right, as if she was looking over your shoulder.　　　　　　　　　（　　）

4. In order for the viewers to feel they are being looked at, the person portrayed must look at them at a gaze angle of 0 degrees.　　　　　　　　　（　　）

5. As the gaze angle increases, you will lose the impression of being looked at.

（　　）

B 以下は記事の要約です。適切な語を空所に書き入れ、音声を聞いて答えを確認しましょう。　　🎧 DL 04　　💿 CD1-18

The Mona Lisa effect is the ($^{1.}$ **n**　　　　　　） that no matter where you move around the room, the eyes of Mona Lisa look ($^{2.}$ **d**　　　　　） at you. German researchers recently conducted an experiment on the painting to ($^{3.}$ **d**　　　　　） if the Mona Lisa effect is real or not. The reply from 24 ($^{4.}$ **p**　　　　　） was that the painting was looking to the ($^{5.}$ **r**　　　　　） at an average angle of 15.4 degrees. This is similar to having someone trying to look over your ($^{6.}$ **s**　　　　　）. The experiment does not doubt the ($^{7.}$ **e**　　　　　） of the Mona Lisa effect; people can feel like they're being looked at from both photographs and paintings if the person portrayed looks ($^{8.}$ **s**　　　　　） ahead out of the image. If Mona Lisa is not looking at you, but looking over your shoulder, you may ($^{9.}$ **q**　　　　　） who is standing right behind you.

Read Better, Understand More!

句読点（コロン、セミコロン、ダッシュ）

句読点（punctuation）の役割を理解すると、英語の文章が速く正確に読めるようになります。次に来る文の内容を予測することができるからです。

ダッシュ（—）　その前の部分をさらに説明するときに用いられます。

例：the Mona Lisa effect—the notion that no matter where art-lovers move around the room …

また、ダッシュがペアで用いられると、丸かっこ（　）と同様に、2つのダッシュに挟まれた情報が付加的なもので文全体の理解に不可欠ではないことを示します。

コロン（:）　ダッシュと同様に前の部分の説明に用いられるほか、具体例をリストアップするときにも使われます。

例：Sheehan outlines several good bedtime habits in his Q&A with *ASU Now*: Refrain from using your phone or watching TV directly before bed, don't over-eat prior to bedtime, and keep your room at a comfortable temperature.（Unit 3）

セミコロン（;）　2つの文を結ぶand（並列）やbut（相反）の代わりに用いられます。（ピリオドで2つの文にしたくはないが、カンマよりも強く区切りたいときに使われます。）

例：These sing-a-longs can last for hours, and males in a given population are known to transmit tunes to one another; they add their own twists to the song, which are then picked up by other males.（Unit 14）

Exercise　次の空所にダッシュ、コロン、セミコロンの中から適切なものを選び書き入れましょう。

1. The Mona Lisa is famous for two things（　）her mysterious smile and her fixed gaze.
2. The Mona Lisa is known in Italy as La Gioconda（　）it is believed to be a portrait of Lisa del Giocondo.
3. The Mona Lisa was painted by DaVinci（　）one of the greatest artists in history.

After You Read

A　会話を聞き、空所を埋めましょう。その後、会話をペアで練習しましょう。

Sarah: You bought a poster of Madonna again?

Daniel: Come on. This is different from other posters. [1.] _____ and follow me no matter where I move around my room. It's amazing.

Sarah: That's not very strange. It's a well-known phenomenon [2.] _____ _____. But interestingly, scientists found out that the Mona Lisa itself [3.] _____.

Daniel: I know. The key to this effect is the gaze angle at which the portrayed person looks at you. If the gaze angle is 0 degrees, you feel like [4.] _____ _____. But I don't care about the scientific explanation. I'm so happy to feel that Madonna looks at me and I am [5.] _____.

Sarah: Good for you!

B　あなた自身の意見を考え、クラスメートと話し合いましょう。

1. Have you ever experienced the Mona Lisa effect? If so, when and where?

2. It is said that actors shouldn't look at the camera, because they would spoil the illusion that the events were real. Can you explain this based on the Mona Lisa effect?

Behind the Scenes　モナリザのモデル

現在パリのルーブル美術館に展示されているモナリザは 1503 年～ 1519 年頃にレオナルド・ダ・ヴィンチが製作したと言われています。16 世紀のイタリア人芸術家ヴァザーリの著書に「レオナルドは、フランチェスコ・デル・ジョコンドから妻リザの肖像画制作の依頼を受けた」との記載があるところから、この作品が「モナ・リザ」とよばれるようになりました。「モナ・リザ」が 1911 年にイタリア人の泥棒に盗まれた際は、フランスの詩人アポリネールが疑われて投獄され、ピカソも警察で尋問されるという事態になりましたが、2 年後に無事モナリザはルーブルに戻ったのでした。

Unit 3

Nearly One-Third of Americans Sleep Fewer Than Six Hours Per Night

睡眠は体と心の健康にとって重要です。不足すると、まず集中力が続かない、イライラするなどの初期症状になって現れ、長期的には体重増加、免疫力の低下、さらには糖尿病や心臓病などのリスクが高まるとされています。現代に生きる私たちの睡眠は足りているのでしょうか。アメリカで行われた調査の結果が発表されました。

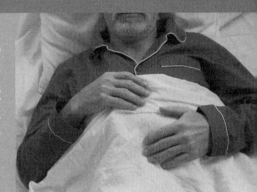

Before You Read

A 日本語の意味に合うように、空所に適切な語を語群から選んで書きましょう。語群には1つ余分なものがあります。

1. 睡眠が足りないと自己申告した　　　　self-reported a (　　　　　) of zzz's
2. 調査結果は気になる傾向を反映している
   the findings (　　　　) a worrying trend
3. 推奨される7〜8時間の睡眠を享受する
   (　　　　　) a recommended seven to eight hours of sleep
4. このノルマを達成することができない　fail to (　　　　) this quota
5. 蓄積された睡眠不足の影響
   the (　　　　) effects of sleep deprivation

| reflect | enjoy | poverty | built-up | meet | survey |

B 下線部の英語の意味として適切な日本語を空所に書きましょう。

1. the number is on the rise　　　　　その数は (　　　　　) いる
2. the likelihood of getting into an accident　事故に遭遇する (　　　　)
3. an increase in race-related discrimination
   人種に関連した (　　　　　) の増加
4. outline several good bedtime habits
   いくつかの良い就寝前の (　　　　　) についてまとめる
5. refrain from using your phone　　　　電話を使用するのを (　　　　　)

19

Reading

Notes

1 The number of Americans sleeping six hours or fewer each night is on the rise. According to a new survey of nearly 400,000 individuals' sleep patterns, 32.9 percent of respondents self-reported a poverty of zzz's in 2017, up from
5 28.6 percent of respondents in 2004.

2 The findings, published in the journal *Sleep*, reflect a worrying trend of national sleep deprivation, specifically among African-American and Hispanic respondents. As Rodrigo Pérez Ortega writes for *Science News*, both groups
10 report higher rates of inadequate sleep than their white counterparts.

3 Of those polled in 2017, 40.9 percent of African-Americans, 32.9 percent of Hispanics and 30.9 percent of Caucasians said they typically slept fewer than six hours per
15 night. The rapid increase evident in these figures—up 6.5 percentage points amongst African-Americans and 7 percent amongst Hispanics from 2004—means these groups are not only suffering from a more severe sleep deficit, "but at a faster rate over time," says study co-author and
20 University of Southern California gerontologist Jennifer Ailshire. From 2004 to 2017, the comparable percentage of Caucasians reporting so-called "short sleep"—six hours or fewer a night—increased by about 2 percent.

4 "Poor sleep is a canary in the coal mine," Ailshire tells
25 *USC News*' Jenesse Miller. "We will see worse health outcomes as a result.

5 Per the National Sleep Foundation, adults aged 18 to 64 should sleep between seven to nine hours per night. Adults over 65 can skim off an hour, enjoying a recom-
30 mended seven to eight hours of sleep. But many Americans regularly fail to meet this quota, leaving them vulnerable to short-term consequences such as an inability to concentrate, mood swings and issues with memory. On a day-to-

Notes:
zzz 寝ること、眠り

Sleep 英国オックスフォード大学出版局発行のジャーナル
deprivation 欠乏

Science News サイエンスニュース誌（米国の科学雑誌）

counterpart 対応する人（ここでは白人を指す）

amongst ～の間で

University of Southern California 南カリフォルニア大学
gerontologist 老人［年］学者

a canary in the coal mine 警告、危険の前触れ
USC News 南カリフォルニア大学が提供しているニュースサイト

the National Sleep Foundation 国立睡眠財団

skim off an hour 一時間削る

mood swing 気分変動

day basis, a lack of sleep can also raise the likelihood of get-
35 ting into an accident or engaging in conflicts at work and
at home. Over time, the built-up effects of sleep deprivation
may lead to weight gain, a weakened immune system that
increases the risk of developing diabetes and heart conditions, and even dementia."

40 **6** Lead study author Connor Sheehan, a demographer
at Arizona State University, tells *ASU Now* that the rise in
short sleep may stem from increased stress levels and an
uptick in smartphone usage before bedtime. While Sheehan
says that the study controlled for income and education
45 variables, he speculates "it's possible that an increase in
race-related discrimination, police violence and focus on
deportation from 2013 to 2017 had an effect" on African-
American and Hispanic participants.

7 Sheehan outlines several good bedtime habits in his
50 Q&A with *ASU Now*: Refrain from using your phone or
watching TV directly before bed, don't over-eat prior to bedtime, and keep your room at a comfortable temperature.
Most importantly, he says, make your bed a space dedicated
to sleep rather than a spot your brain associates with day-
55 time activities.

immune 免疫の

diabetes 糖尿病

dementia 認知症

demographer 人口統計学者

Arizona State University
アリゾナ州立大学
ASU Now
アリゾナ州立大学が提供してい
るニュースサイト
stem from ～ ～から生じる
uptick 増加

deportation 国外退去

Comprehension Questions

A 記事の内容に一致するものには T（True）、一致しないものには F（False）を空所に書き入れましょう。

1. More than thirty percent of Americans sleep fewer than six hours per night, and this figure has not changed for decades. (　　)
2. African-Americans and Hispanics are not only suffering from a more serious sleep deprivation than Caucasians but more rapidly. (　　)
3. The National Sleep Foundation recommends that adults aged between 18 and 64 need less hours of sleep than those who are over 65. (　　)
4. According to a demographer at Arizona State University, increased stress levels may play a role in the rise in short sleep. (　　)
5. Connor Sheehan notes it's important to keep your bed exclusively for sleeping.

(　　)

B 以下は記事の要約です。適切な語を空所に書き入れ、音声を聞いて答えを確認しましょう。 🎧 DL 06　◎ CD1-27

Nearly (¹· **o**　　　　　　) of Americans now sleep fewer than six hours per night. In particular, African- and Hispanic-Americans report higher rates of (²· **i**　　　　　) sleep than their white (³· **c**　　　　).

The National Sleep Foundation (⁴· **r**　　　　　) that adults aged 18 to 64 should sleep between seven to nine hours per night, and those who are over 65 should sleep between seven to eight hours, but many Americans regularly fail to meet this (⁵· **q**　　　　). Sleep deficit has (⁶· **s**　　　　) consequences including an inability to concentrate, and long-term consequences such as weight gain, a weakened immune system, or even dementia.

To sleep well, it is important not to use your (⁷· **p**　　　　) or watch TV directly before bed, not to (⁸· **o**　　　　) prior to bedtime, to keep your room at a (⁹· **c**　　　　) temperature, and to make your bed a space (¹⁰· **d**　　　) to sleep.

Read Better, Understand More!

数字

科学のニュースや記事に不可欠なもの、それは数字です。主な読み方を以下にまとめました。

整数：1,000(one thousand), 10,000(ten thousand), 100,000(one hundred thousand), 1,000,000(one million),1,000,000,000(one billion)

少数：0.1(zero point one), 0.11(zero point one one), -0.007(minus zero point zero zero seven), -12.9(minus twelve point nine)

分数：$\frac{1}{2}$(a[one] half), $\frac{1}{3}$(a[one] third), $\frac{1}{4}$(a[one] quarter), $\frac{2}{3}$(two thirds), $\frac{b}{c}$(b over c)

分数は英語では最初に分子（基数）、次に分母（序数）の順に読みます。分子が1以外の場合、分母は複数になります。ただし$\frac{1}{2}$は one second ではなく a[one] half です。$\frac{1}{4}$は a[one] quarter のほかに one fourth も使われます。数字でない分数には over を使います。

単位：℃ (degree Celsius), %(percent), m(meter), g(gram), kg(kilogram)

％ を除く単位は前に来る数字に応じて複数になります。例えば 1.5 m は one point five meters です。では 0℃はどうでしょうか。0 degrees Celsius と読みます。ゼロも複数扱いになることに注意しましょう。一方、％ は前にどのような数字がきても複数にはなりません。例えば 20％ は twenty percent[per cent] です。ただし「百分率」という意味で percent を使うときには percents という複数形が存在します。この意味の percent は percentage と言い換えることもできます。つまり、15％(15 percent) や 55％(55 percent) 自体は百分率なので、これら一つ一つは a percentage[percent] であり、これら2つをまとめれば percentages[percents] となるのです。

Exercise 次の数字と文の読み方を単位も含めて書きましょう。

例：- 159℃　　　　　→　minus one hundred fifty-nine degrees Celsius

1. 10,000 m　　　→　_____

2. 12.89 g　　　　→　_____

3. $\frac{3}{5}$ of 20 is 12.　→　_____

After You Read

A 会話を聞き、空所を埋めましょう。その後、会話をペアで練習しましょう。

🎧 DL 07   ◎ CD1-28

Ann: You look so sleepy! You stayed up late last night again, didn't you?

Glenn: No, on the contrary, I went to bed quite early, but I ¹·＿＿＿＿＿＿＿＿
＿＿＿＿＿＿＿＿＿＿＿＿＿.

Ann: Same here. I'm suffering from ²·＿＿＿＿＿＿＿＿＿＿＿＿＿.

Glenn: As I couldn't sleep last night, I searched the web and found an article titled
"25 ³·＿＿＿＿＿＿＿＿＿＿＿＿＿＿＿＿", but it didn't help.

Ann: I'm afraid that's the last thing you should do. Blue light can affect your
sleep. They say we should ⁴·＿＿＿＿＿＿＿＿＿＿＿＿＿＿＿
＿＿＿＿＿＿＿＿ right before bed.

Glenn: All right. The next time I have a hard time getting to sleep, I'll read
"Finnegans Wake"*. Then, I'll ⁵·＿＿＿＿＿＿＿＿＿＿＿＿＿＿＿
＿＿＿＿＿＿＿!

Ann: That might help. I think I'll try to listen to relaxing music before bedtime.

*__Finnegans Wake__：アイルランドの小説家ジェイムズ・ジョイスの最後の小説であり、非常に難解な作品として有名。

B あなた自身の意見を考え、クラスメートと話し合いましょう。

1. How many hours do you sleep every night? Are you satisfied with the current
situation?

2. What do you do when you cannot fall asleep? What will help you sleep better?
Discuss ways to improve your sleep.

Behind the Scenes　　適切な量の睡眠をとることが重要

睡眠不足が体に悪いということはよく知られていますが、眠り過ぎも体に悪影響がある
ということが最近分かってきました。理想とされる一日7～9時間の睡眠をとっている
被験者とそれより睡眠時間が長い被験者とを比較した研究から指摘された、寝過ぎに伴
う7つのリスクは、次の通りです。
1. 鬱のリスク（2014年の成人の双子の調査から）、2. 脳の機能の低下（2012年の年配の
女性を対象にした調査から）、3. 妊娠しづらくなる（2013年の体外受精を行っている女
性の調査から）、4. 糖尿病のリスク（カナダで実施された6年間の研究から）、5. 体重の
増加（同上）、6. 心臓疾患のリスク（2012年に発表された3000人のデータから）、7. 寿
命が縮む（2010年に精査した16の研究から）

（出典：HuffPost）

Unit 4

There's No Limit on Longevity, But Getting Super Old Is Still Tough

ヒトの寿命には上限があるのでしょうか。これまでの最高齢の記録は 122 歳ですが、人の寿命はその辺が限度とする考えがあります。2016 年に発表された論文もそれを支持するものでしたが、その結果に納得のいかなかった研究者らは、このほどイタリアに住む 3,836 名の長寿者を対象に新たに調査を行い、人の寿命には限界はないとする研究結果をサイエンス誌で報告しました。

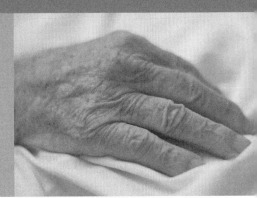

Before You Read

A 日本語の意味に合うように、空所に適切な語を語群から選んで書きましょう。語群には 1 つ余分なものがあります。

1. 長寿の研究では驚くほど意見が分かれる
   the science of longevity is surprisingly (　　　　　)
2. 年齢とともに、私たちが死ぬ確率は指数関数的に増加する
   the odds of dying (　　　　　) exponentially as we age
3. 死亡率の壁　　　　　　　　　　a wall of (　　　　　)
4. 3,836 名の寿命を調べる　　　　look at the (　　　　　) of 3,836 people
5. 出生証明書で年齢を確認する　　(　　　　　) ages by birth certificates

> **verify　grow　research　mortality　lifespans　controversial**

B 下線部の英語の意味として適切な日本語を空所に書きましょう。

1. a limit on human <u>longevity</u>　　　人の（　　　　　）の限界
2. an age we just can't <u>get past</u>　　　私たちが（　　　　　）られない年齢
3. look to <u>statistics</u>　　　（　　　　　）を頼みにする
4. <u>figure out</u> how long people can live
   人々がどれだけ長く生きることができるのか（　　　　　）
5. not everyone is <u>convinced</u> by the data
   皆がそのデータに（　　　　　）わけではない

Reading

Notes

1 Something miraculous happened during the 20th century that rarely gets mentioned along with techno-leaps like the airplane, television, radio, A-bomb and the Internet: due to improved public health, medicine and nutrition
5 the average human lifespan on Earth doubled. The big question now is whether it could double again. Is there a natural biological limit on human longevity, an age we just can't get past? Or, given the right circumstances, could a lucky human give Methuselah a run for his money? Ben
10 Guarino at *The Washington Post* reports that a new study of very old Italians suggests that there isn't a cap on how long a human can keep going in this mortal coil.

2 The science of longevity is surprisingly controversial, mainly because there are so few people of extreme old
15 age—defined at 110 years or older—around to study. So researchers look to statistics to try and figure out how long people can live. Guarino reports that in 1825, actuary Benjamin Gompertz put forth the idea that the odds of dying grow exponentially as we age. Further research bears that
20 out. Between the age of 30 and 80, the odds of dying double every 8 years. What happens after that, however, is not completely figured out.

3 According to a controversial study released in 2016, which analyzed data from 40 different countries, the aver-
25 age person could make it to 115 with the right genes and interventions, and a few genetic superstars would be able to make it to 125. But that was it, they argued. There was a wall of mortality that medicine and positive thinking simply could not overcome.

4 But not everyone is convinced by that data. That's why
30 for the new paper in the journal *Science*, researchers looked at the lifespans of 3,836 people in Italy who reached the age of 105 or older between 2009 and 2015, with their ages ver-

---

miraculous
奇跡的な、驚くべき

give *someone* a run for
one's money
(人) と張り合う
Methuselah
メトセラ (969 歳まで生きたと
される)
The Washington Post
ワシントンポスト紙(米国の新聞)
cap 上限
mortal coil 騒々しいこの世

actuary 保険数理士
Benjamin Gompertz
ベンジャミン・ゴンペルツ。成
人後は死亡率が年齢の指数関数
になることをゴンペルツ関数で
表した。
put forth ~ ~を発表する
odds 確率
exponentially 指数関数的に
bear ~ out ~を実証する

make it やり遂げる

intervention
(病気などの) 治療処置
that is it それでおしまい

Science
サイエンス誌。アメリカ科学振
興協会によって発行されている
学術雑誌。

ified by birth certificates. What they found is that the Gom-
35 pertz law goes a little haywire around the century mark.
According to a press release, a 90-year-old woman has a 15
percent chance of dying in the next year, and an estimated
six years left to live. At age 95, the chance of dying per year
jumps to 24 percent. At the age of 105, the chance of dying
40 makes another leap to 50 percent. But then, surprisingly,
it levels off, even past 110. In other words, at least statistically, each year some lucky person could flip the coin of life,
and if it comes up heads every time, they could live beyond
115 or 125.

45 **5** "Our data tell us that there is no fixed limit to the human lifespan yet in sight," senior author Kenneth Wachter
of UC Berkeley says in the release. "Not only do we see
mortality rates that stop getting worse with age, we see
them getting slightly better over time."

Notes

go haywire　混乱する、狂う

level off　横ばいになる
statistically　統計的に
flip　はじく

in sight　見えて

UC Berkeley
カリフォルニア大学バークレー校

Comprehension Questions

A 記事の内容に一致するものには T（True）、一致しないものには F（False）を空所に書き入れましょう。

1. During the 20th century there were many technological advances including the airplane, television, radio, Internet, etc. (   )

2. The science of longevity is controversial, partly because there are so few people of extreme old age to study, and partly because we cannot conduct experiments on human subjects. (   )

3. In a controversial study released in 2016, they concluded that there is a wall of mortality that people cannot overcome. (   )

4. The new paper published in the journal *Science* showed that the chance of dying does not increase after the age of 105, suggesting that if a person is lucky enough, he can live beyond 115 or even 125. (   )

5. The paper published in the journal *Science* shows that human mortality rates stop increasing at late ages but never decrease. (   )

B 以下は記事の要約です。適切な語を空所に書き入れ、音声を聞いて答えを確認しましょう。　　🎧 DL 08　　💿 CD1-34

In 1825, Benjamin Gompertz put (1. **f**   ) the idea that the (2. **o**   ) of dying grow (3. **e**   ) with age. Between the age of 30 and 80, the chance of dying (4. **d**   ) every 8 years. What follows after that is not precisely (5. **f**   ) out. In 2016, data from 40 different countries were analyzed and the researchers concluded that the (6. **a**   ) limit for the human lifespan is 115, and the maximum lifespan is 125. Then the researchers who were not (7. **c**   ) by the data looked at the lifespans of 3,836 people in Italy who reached the age of 105 (8. **o**   ) older. They found that the chance of dying (9. **l**   ) off after the age of 105, (10. **s**   ) that a lucky person could live (11. **b**   ) 115 or 125.

Read Better, Understand More!

数量表現　1

科学の世界では定性的な表現（非常に重い、とても優れている）よりも定量的な表現（重さが 100kg である、1 番優秀である）が好まれます。つまり数字を使って具体的に説明することが重要なのです。本文で使われた表現を挙げてみます。

110 years or older　　　　　　　　「110 歳以上」
between the age of 30 and 80　　　「30 歳から 80 歳まで（の間）」
double every 8 years　　　　　　　「8 年毎に倍になる」
reached the age of 105 or older between 2009 and 2015
「2009 年から 2015 年までに 105 歳以上の年齢に到達した」

more than、less than の使い方に注意しましょう。「110 歳以上」は上記のように 110 years or older で、older than 110 years と表現すると「110 歳を超える」という意味になり 110 歳は含まれません。同様に less than 10kg は「10kg 未満」を表すため 10kg は含まれません。

「A から B まで」は本文のように between A and B と表現することもできますし from A to B という表現も可能です。

「2 倍になる」は動詞 double で、「半分になる」は動詞 halve で表します。例えば「確率は 5 年毎に半分になる」は Odds halve every 5 years. となります。

Exercise　日本語の意味に合うように、空所に適切な語を書きましょう。

例: 1 歳未満の赤ちゃん　→　a baby under[younger than] one year old
1. 23 kg を越える重量超過手荷物
    →　overweight baggage weighing (　　　　　)(　　　　　) 23 kg
2. 液の量が半分になるまでコトコト煮ます。
    →　Simmer until the liquid (　　　　　) in quantity.
3. 6 歳から 12 歳までの子供は半額、6 歳未満は無料です。
    →　Children aged (　　　　) 6 (　　　　　) 12 years pay 50% of the
    ticket price. Free of charge if the child is (　　　　)(　　　　　) 6
    years old.

After You Read

A 会話を聞き、空所を埋めましょう。その後、会話をペアで練習しましょう。

🎧 DL 09　　💿 CD1-35

Robert: Maya, do you think ¹·_____?

Maya: Well … I would rather say yes. But why do you ask such a question all of a sudden?

Robert: I watched a TV program, "Telomeres: Unlocking the Mystery of Cell Division and Aging" and ²·_____.
Telomeres are in our bodies and closely related to cell aging. The longer the telomeres are, the slower the ageing process is. So we can live longer. We can even ³·_____.

Maya: You mean, we can live longer and better by lengthening our telomeres?

Robert: Yes, ⁴·_____, managing chronic stress, eating a telomere-protective diet, and sleeping well. There are people called centenarians* or supercentenarians**. I would like to be one of them!

Maya: I don't want to ⁵·_____. It must be so hard to live with your old body!

*centenarian：100 歳から 109 歳までの人
**supercentenarian：110 歳以上の人

B あなた自身の意見を考え、クラスメートと話し合いましょう。

1. Do you think there is a limit on longevity?
2. Do you want to be a centenarian or a supercentenarian?

Behind the Scenes　テロメア（命の回数券）

私たちの体細胞の中にある染色体の端にはテロメアと呼ばれる部分があり、細胞分裂を繰り返すたびに短くなっていきます。テロメアの長さがある一定の値（ヘイフリック限界）を下回るようになると、それ以上細胞が分裂しなくなるため、テロメアは別名「命の回数券」ともよばれているのです。ヘイフリック限界とは細胞の分裂回数の限界のことで、ヒトでは50、そこから計算される最大寿命は約120年で、これまでの最長寿の年齢を裏付けています。

Unit 5

Chinese City Wants to Launch Fake Moon to Illuminate Its Streets

夜空を見上げるとそこには月が2つ。まるでSF小説のようですが、近い将来は現実になっているかもしれません。中国では、人工の月を打ち上げて成都（四川省）を明るく照らし出そうという計画が進められています。

Before You Read

A 日本語の意味に合うように、空所に適切な語を語群から選んで書きましょう。語群には1つ余分なものがあります。

1. ベルサイユ宮殿の鏡の間の宇宙版を心に描く

   (　　　　　　　　) a cosmic version of Versailles' Hall of Mirrors
2. このアイデアにヒントを得た　　　　(　　　　　　　　) by the idea
3. 本物の月の8倍の明るさ

   eight (　　　　　　) brighter than the real moon
4. 壮大な計画を公表する　　　　　(　　　　　　　　) the singular plan
5. 衛星の仕様を始めとする詳細　　　details including satellite (　　　　　　)

> **inspired　times　powered　unveil　envision　specifications**

B 下線部の英語の意味として適切な日本語を空所に書きましょう。

1. a precise illumination range　　　(　　　　　　　　) 照明の範囲
2. the satellite has been in the testing phase

   この衛星は試験（　　　　　　）にあった
3. adverse effects on wildlife and astronomical observation

   野生生物や天文観測に対する（　　　　　　）
4. transform night into day　　　　夜を昼に（　　　　　　）
5. the underlying concept embraced by the experiment

   この実験が（　　　　　）基本的な考え

Reading

CD1-36 ~ CD1-43

Notes

1 A French artist once envisioned a cosmic version of Versailles' famed Hall of Mirrors, reportedly proposing the creation of an artificial moon powered by a necklace of mirrors that would reflect light back onto the streets of Paris.
5 This bold plan never came to fruition, but as Chinese news outlet *The People's Daily* reports, an illumination satellite inspired by the idea may brighten the streets of Chengdu as soon as 2020.

2 The satellite, which is also known as an artificial
10 moon, will be able to illuminate a roughly 6- to 50-mile wide stretch of the southwestern Chinese city with light eight times brighter than that of the real moon. If all goes well, the fake moon will produce enough light to replace Chengdu's street lamps. According to *The Asia Times*,
15 Chengdu's artificial moon will feature a highly reflective coating that reflects the sun's rays via solar panel-like wings. The angles of these wings can be tweaked in order to create a precise illumination range of several dozen meters.

3 Wu Chunfeng, head of the Chengdu Aerospace Science
20 and Technology Microelectronics System Research Institute, unveiled the singular plan at a national mass innovation and entrepreneurship event held last week. Citing the imagined French necklace of mirrors as the impetus for the project, Chunfeng explained that the technology behind
25 the satellite has been in the testing phase for years but is finally near completion.

4 Although Chengdu, capital of China's Sichuan province, is set to be the man-made moon's focus, astronomers across the globe will reportedly be able to spot the satel-
30 lite's glow as they search the night sky. Giulio Calenne of Chinese commerce outlet *CIFnews* writes that the idea has raised concerns amongst those who fear the artificial light could have adverse effects on wildlife and astronomical ob-

cosmic 宇宙の

famed 有名な
reportedly
伝えられるところによれば

come to fruition 実現する
news outlet 報道機関
The People's Daily
人民日報。中国共産党中央委員会の機関誌。
illumination 照明
Chengdu 成都

a stretch of ~
~の範囲にわたり

The Asia Times
香港を拠点とする日刊のオンライン新聞
reflective 反射性の

tweak 微調整する

Chengdu Aerospace
Science and Technology
Microelectronics System
Research Institute
成都航空宇宙科学電子技術システム研究所
singular 並外れた
entrepreneurship
起業家精神
impetus 刺激、誘発要因

Sichuan province 四川省

astronomer 天文学者

CIFnews
2013年に創立されたCBEC（国境を越えた電子商取引）専門の中国メディア
astronomical 天文（学）の

32

servation.

35 **5** Kang Weimin, director of the Harbin Institute of Technology's School of Aerospace, refutes these concerns, telling Calenne that the satellite will produce a dusk-like glow far too faint to transform night into day.

6 For now, details on the proposed moon—including fur-
40 ther satellite specifications, cost and launch date—remain scarce. As *Fortune*'s Don Reisinger notes, Chengdu officials hope the project will generate a financial windfall, allowing the city to cut electricity costs and attract tourists.

7 This isn't the first time researchers have tried to illu-
45 minate the skies with artificial rays. *The Telegraph*'s Joseph Archer reports that Russian scientists launched a mirror-equipped spacecraft designed to brighten Siberia's sun-deprived streets back in 1999.

8 The device, dubbed Znamya 2, collapsed soon after
50 take-off and was subsequently abandoned. Still, the underlying concept embraced by the experiment—which *The New York Times* described at the time as a test of "the feasibility of illuminating points on Earth with light equivalent to that of several full moons"—remains an enticing prospect.
55 And, by 2020, it may even become reality.

Notes

Harbin Institute of
Technology's School of
Aerospace
ハルビン工業大学航空宇宙学部
refute 反論する
dusk 夕暮れ

Fortune
米タイム社が発行するビジネス
誌
windfall 思いがけない収入

The Telegraph
英国の新聞デイリーテレグラフ
のオンライン版

spacecraft 宇宙船

dub ニックネームをつける

underlying 基本的な

The New York Times
ニューヨークタイムズ紙（米国
の新聞）
feasibility 実行可能性

enticing 魅力的な

Comprehension Questions

A 記事の内容に一致するものには T （True）、一致しないものには F （False） を空所に書き入れましょう。

1. The illumination satellite would reflect sunlight down to Chengdu, creating a glow about eighty times brighter than that of the moon. (　　)

2. The angles of the satellite's wings can be adjusted to concentrate the light on a precise location. (　　)

3. The fake moon can be observed only from Chengdu. (　　)

4. Whether the light from the fake moon will have a negative impact on wildlife and astronomical observation is controversial. (　　)

5. Prior to the Chinese attempt, French and Russian researchers have tried to illuminate the skies with artificial rays. (　　)

B 以下は記事の要約です。適切な語を空所に書き入れ、音声を聞いて答えを確認しましょう。　　🎧 DL 10　　💿 CD1-44

China is planning to launch a fake moon, or an (¹· **a**　　　　) moon, to illuminate Chengdu. The brightness of the (²· **s**　　　　) is (³· **e**　　　　) times that of the real moon, and it will be able to light an area with a diameter of about 6 to 50 miles. This project was inspired by a French artist's idea — a (⁴· **n**　　　　) of mirrors.

Although Chengdu is set to be the (⁵· **f**　　　　) of the satellite, which can be precisely adjusted in order to create an illumination range of several dozen meters, there are (⁶· **c**　　　　) amongst those who fear the artificial light could have (⁷· **a**　　　　) effects on wildlife and (⁸· **a**　　　　) observation.

Chengdu officials hope the artificial moon could replace (⁹· **s**　　　　) lights, and cut electricity (¹⁰· **c**　　　　).

Read Better, Understand More!

数量表現　2

比較の表現でも、much や far を使った *A* is much[far] brighter than *B.* という文よりも、本文の例のように eight times などと数字を使う方がより科学的（定量的）です。

1. light (which is) eight times brighter than that of the real moon
   「本物の月の８倍の明るさの光」
2. light (which is) equivalent to that of several full moons
   「数個の満月に相当する光」

比較の際は、同じ物同士を比較することが重要です。つまり、ここでは衛星の発する「光」を月の「光」と比較しているわけです。

1. では brighter than のあとに、2. では equivalent to のあとに、それぞれ that が置かれていますが、この that は light という語を繰り返す代わりに用いられている代名詞です。日本語では「本物の月の８倍の明るさ」「数個の満月に相当する」と表現するので、つられて eight times brighter than the real moon や equivalent to several full moons などとしないように注意しましょう。

Exercise 次の文に（　　　）内の数字を入れて、より科学的な表現にしましょう。

1. He is much younger than I.（20 歳）
   → _____

2. I always sleep a little longer than my wife.（１時間）
   → _____

3. I used to weigh more than I do now.（10kg）
   → _____

After You Read

A 会話を聞き、空所を埋めましょう。その後、会話をペアで練習しましょう。

🎧 DL 011   💿 CD1-45

Brian: Mary, I'm planning ¹._____.
Will you come with me?

Mary: You always surprise me! What are you going to do there?

Brian: I've just read an article about China's fake moon. They will ²._____
_____ in order to illuminate the streets of
Chengdu.

Mary: That's unbelievable! You mean we'll be able to see ³._____
_____?

Brian: Yeah. I can hardly wait to see them ⁴._____
_____.

Mary: Gee, that's really romantic. The image of two moons in the sky reminds me
of the novel *1Q84** by Haruki Murakami.

Brian: But there is a downside to this project. Some people are pointing out that
⁵._____, particularly
nocturnal animals**, as well as people.

＊**1Q84**：2009 年から 2010 年にかけて出版された村上春樹の長編小説。現実の世界（1984 年の世界）と微妙に異なる（パラレルワール
ド）月が 2 個存在する 1Q84 年の世界が登場する。

＊＊**nocturnal**：夜行性の

B あなた自身の意見を考え、クラスメートと話し合いましょう。

1. How do you find China's idea of launching a fake moon?

2. Do you think the artificial light will have adverse effects on wildlife?

Behind the Scenes　人工衛星ラッシュ

人類初の人工衛星はソビエト連邦が 1957 年 10 月 4 日に打ち上げたスプートニク（ロシ
ア語で「衛星」の意味）1 号でした。直径 58cm のアルミニウム製の球からなる、重量
83.6kg のこの衛星は、高度が下がって翌年 1 月 4 日に大気圏に再突入し消滅するまでの
92 日間、地球の回りを 96.2 分で周回し続けたのでした。それから 60 年あまりがたち、
衛星の種類や数はどんどん増え続けています。これまでに世界各国で打ち上げられた人
工衛星の数は 2017 年 2 月時点で 7,600 機を超え、地上に回収されたものや落下したもの
を除くと現在 4,400 機以上の人工衛星が地球を周回しています（出典：国連宇宙部）。

Unit 6

Doctors "Grow" Ear for Transplant in Patient's Forearm

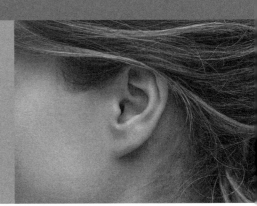

事故で片方の耳（外耳）を丸ごと失ってしまったら？　本物そっくりのエピテーゼ（人工の耳）を装着するという選択肢もあります。しかし、最新の医療技術のおかげで、新しい耳を患者の腕に生やし、それを移植することも可能になったのです。

Before You Read

A 日本語の意味に合うように、空所に適切な語を語群から選んで書きましょう。語群には1つ余分なものがあります。

1. 患者の失われた耳を再建する　　　（　　　　　　　　）a patient's lost ear
2. 肋骨の軟骨を使って新しい耳を彫り上げる
   （　　　　　　　　）a new ear from rib cartilage
3. 患者を形成外科に紹介する　　　　refer the patient to (　　　　　　) surgery
4. この手術は古くから行われている　the procedure has long (　　　　　　)
5. そのような血管成長は体のあらゆる箇所で可能なわけではない
   such blood vessel (　　　　　　) isn't possible everywhere in the body

> **plastic　development　stitch　sculpt　reconstruct　roots**

B 下線部の英語の意味として適切な日本語を空所に書きましょう。

1. <u>implant</u> it under the tissues of the patient's forearm
   その患者の前腕の組織の下にそれを（　　　　　　　　）
2. <u>foster</u> blood vessel growth　　　血管の成長を（　　　　　　　　）
3. the vehicle <u>flips</u> across the road　車は道路の向こう側まで（　　　　　　　　）
4. she continued to <u>suffer</u> from insecurities about her appearance
   彼女は引き続き自分の外見への自信喪失に（　　　　　　　　）
5. more patients could probably <u>benefit</u> from the procedure
   さらに多くの患者がこの手術から（　　　　　　　　）ことができるだろう

Reading

CD1-46 ~ CD1-54

Notes

1　To successfully reconstruct a patient's lost ear, doctors at William Beaumont Army Medical Center in El Paso, Texas sculpted a new one from rib cartilage and implanted it under the tissues of the patient's forearm to foster blood
5　vessel growth.

2　The patient is Army private Shamika Burrage, who lost her ear in a car accident two years ago, reports Neel V. Patel for *Popular Science*. Burrage was returning from leave when her car's front tire blew, sending the vehicle
10　flipping across the road and ejecting her from her seat.

3　Burrage, now 21, spent several months in rehabilitation after the accident but sought counseling when she continued to suffer from insecurities about her appearance. "I didn't feel comfortable with the way I looked so the pro-
15　vider referred me to plastic surgery," Burrage says.

4　During the reconstruction process, surgeons reopened Burrage's hearing canal to restore her hearing and implanted the vascularized ear in its rightful place. She will require two more surgeries to complete the process, but is
20　currently faring well, according to a U.S. Army statement on the procedure.

5　"The whole goal is that by the time she's done with all this, it looks good, it's sensate, and in five years if somebody doesn't know her they won't notice," says Lt. Col. Owen
25　Johnson III, the chief of plastic and reconstructive surgery at the facility, in the statement.

6　Though a first for Army plastic surgeons, the procedure has long roots in medical practices, Patel reports. Since the early 20th century, doctors have reconstructed parts of
30　ears in people suffering from congenital deformities using a technique that involves harvesting rib cartilage from the chest, sculpting it into the shape of an ear and implanting it under the skin where the ear is normally placed.

William Beaumont Army Medical Center ウィリアム・ボーモント陸軍医療センター
rib　肋骨
cartilage　軟骨
tissue　組織
forearm　前腕
blood vessel　血管
private　兵卒

Popular Science ポピュラーサイエンス誌。科学技術記事を掲載している米国の季刊誌。
eject　外に出す

insecurity　自信喪失、不安感

refer ～ to ...
(患者)を(専門医など)に紹介する

hearing canal　耳管

vascularize　血管を新生する
rightful　本来あるべき

fare well　元気にやっていく

sensate　感覚がある

Lt. Col.
(Lieutenant Colonel の略で)中佐

medical practice　医療行為

congenital　先天的な
deformity　奇形

7   As Patel writes, the second stage of the latest ear
35 transplant, known as microvascular free tissue transfer,
only became popular in the late 1990s. By stitching the implanted tissue to blood vessels, doctors can help it develop
into "healthy, functioning tissue in a new area," Patrick
Byrne, the director of the Division of Facial Plastic and Re-
40 constructive Surgery at Johns Hopkins University School
of Medicine who pioneered this method, tells Patel.

8   But such blood vessel development isn't possible everywhere in the body—including the normal position of ears,
Patel reports. In Burrage's case, doctors encouraged this
45 vascularization by initially implanting the ear on her forearm, where there is an artery and vein to support growth.
"[The ear] will have fresh arteries, fresh veins and even a
fresh nerve so she'll be able to feel it," Johnson says in the
statement.

50 **9**   While this procedure is rare, Byrne tells Patel that
more patients who experience severe damage to the struc-
tures of the ear could probably benefit from it.

microvascular 微小血管の
free tissue transfer
遊離組織移植

Division of Facial Plas-
tic and Reconstructive
Surgery at Johns Hop-
kins University School of
Medicine
ジョンズ・ホプキンス大学医学
部顔面形成外科

artery 動脈
vein 静脈

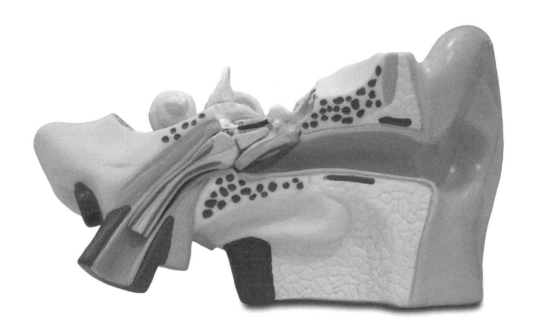

Comprehension Questions

A 記事の内容に一致するものには T（True）、一致しないものには F（False）を空所に書き入れましょう。

1. Doctors at William Beaumont Army Medical Center implanted an ear-shaped rib cartilage on a patient's forearm to grow an ear for transplant. (　　)
2. Burrage was involved in a car accident with a pedestrian. (　　)
3. The reason why Burrage decided to have ear reconstruction surgery is that she wanted to restore hearing. (　　)
4. The surgeons hope that the procedure will restore sensation to the ear. (　　)
5. Ear reconstruction surgery has a long history, particularly in the treatment of ear deformities. (　　)

B 以下は記事の要約です。適切な語を空所に書き入れ、音声を聞いて答えを確認しましょう。　　　　 DL 12　　 CD1-55

　　Two years ago, an Army (¹· p　　　　　　) lost her ear in a car accident and went through (²· r　　　　　　) during several months after the accident. She was suffering from (³· i　　　　　　) about her appearance and decided to have (⁴· r　　　　　) surgery. First, doctors (⁵· s　　　　　) a new ear from rib (⁶· c　　　　　) and (⁷· i　　　　　) it under the tissues of her forearm to foster blood vessel (⁸· g　　　　　). Then they reopened her hearing canal to (⁹· r　　　　　) her hearing and implanted the (¹⁰· v　　　　　) ear in its rightful place. She will require two more surgeries to (¹¹· c　　　　　) the process; in the future, her ear will have not only fresh arteries and veins but also a fresh nerve, so she'll be able to feel it. Doctors hope that in five years if somebody doesn't know her they won't (¹²· n　　　　　) the fact that one of her ears was reconstructed.

Read Better, Understand More!

$$\boxed{\text{前置詞}}$$

前置詞は前後の単語の関係を規定するという働きを持っており、細かなニュアンスまで英文を正確に読みとるためには、前置詞に気を配ることが重要です。例えば、本文の doctors <u>at</u> William Beaumont …と the director <u>of</u> the Division of Facial Plastic …という記載ですが、at も of も日本語に訳せば「の」になりますが、at には「その場所で働いている」、of には「その組織に所属している」というニュアンスがあるのです。

場所を示す前置詞：in、on、at
in は広がりをもったもの「の中に」、on は面や線に接して「の上に」、at は狭い領域「に」、それぞれ存在するときに使われます。
例： doctors <u>at</u> William Beaumont Army Medical Center <u>in</u> El Paso
　　El Paso は町なので広い領域を表す in が、William Beaumont Army Medical Center は施設なので狭い領域を表す at が使われています。
例： initially implanting the ear <u>on</u> her forearm
　　前腕に接して、その上にという意味で on が使われています。

時間を示す前置詞：in、during、by
例： <u>in</u> the late 1990s「1990 年代に」
　　<u>During</u> the reconstruction process「再建過程の間に」
　　<u>by</u> the time she's done with all this「彼女がこれを全て終わる頃までに」

Exercise 　図のように三角形（triangle）の中に点 O が、辺（side）の上に点 P が、頂点（vertex）の上に点 Q があります。次の英文の空所に適切な前置詞を書きましょう。

1. Point O is (　　　　　) the triangle.
2. Point P is (　　　　　) the side.
3. Point Q is (　　　　　) the vertex.

After You Read

A 会話を聞き、空所を埋めましょう。その後、会話をペアで練習しましょう。

🎧 DL 13　　◎ CD1-56

Henry: Emma, Uncle Jim ¹. _____ yesterday.

Emma: Oh, what happened?

Henry: He got in a car accident and his finger was severely injured, so he had to ². _____ .

Emma: I'm sorry to hear that. Did the surgery go well? Is he ³. _____ ?

Henry: Yes, everything went very well. Though his finger was ⁴. _____ , he was able to find the severed* finger. And the doctor and his team were ⁵. _____ in microsurgery. The operation he had is called "digit replantation**."

Emma: I understand. When you said he had plastic surgery, I almost mistook it for cosmetic surgery. The terms are confusing … A handsome guy like him doesn't need any though.

***severed**：切断された
****digit replantation**：（切断）指再接着術

B あなた自身の意見を考え、クラスメートと話し合いましょう。

1. Do you agree or disagree to people having cosmetic surgery to improve the way they look?

2. What are the merits and demerits of cosmetic surgery?

Behind the Scenes　　整形外科と形成外科はどう違う？

整形外科（orthopedic surgery）は骨や関節などの骨格系とそれを取り囲む筋肉や神経系からなる「運動器」の機能的な改善を重要視して治療する外科で、背骨と骨盤という体の土台骨と、四肢を主な治療対象にしています。これに対し、形成外科（plastic surgery）は、生まれながらの異常や、病気や怪我などによって身体表面が見目の良くない状態になったのを改善する（治療する）外科で、頭や顔面を含めた体全体を治療対象としています。美容外科（cosmetic surgery）は形成外科の一分野で、容姿を整えることが目的の、いわゆる「美容整形」の手術を行います。（参考：公益社団法人　日本整形外科学会ホームページ）

Unit 7

A German Grocery Chain Is Selling First-Of-Its-Kind "No-Kill" Eggs

ブロイラー業界では、オスのひよこは生まれるとすぐに殺され、動物の餌にされています。もし、ひよこになる前に卵の中で雌雄を判別することができれば、このような残酷な慣習を廃止することができるだろう、という思いが実を結び、世界初の「ノーキル（殺さない）」エッグがこのほどドイツのスーパーから発売されました。

Before You Read

A 日本語の意味に合うように、空所に適切な語を語群から選んで書きましょう。語群には１つ余分なものがあります。

1. 知識のある消費者　　　　　　　　　(　　　　　　　) consumers
2. より持続可能な解決法を見つける　　find a more (　　　　　) solution
3. メスの卵の中に存在するホルモン　　a hormone (　　　　　) in female eggs
4. 卵の性別を決定する　　　　　　　　(　　　　　　　) the sex of the eggs
5. その会社は解決法を探し求める　　　the company (　　　　　) solutions

> **sustainable　determine　seeks　present　knowledgeable　dispose**

B 下線部の英語の意味として適切な日本語を空所に書きましょう。

1. give rise to the world's first no-kill eggs
世界初の殺さない卵を（　　　　　　　）

2. a Dutch company called HatchTech developed a way to mass test
ハッチテック（　　　　　　　　）オランダの会社は大量試験方法を開発した

3. pursue another method of sex identification that involves light
光を用いたもう１つの性別判定法を（　　　　　　　）

4. it keeps us all focused on that goal
それは私たちみんなをその目標に（　　　　　　　）させる

5. end chick culling for good
ひよこの間引きを（　　　　　　　）終わらせる

43

Reading

Notes

1 Male chicks are pretty much useless to the egg and broiler industry; they don't produce eggs and their bodies don't grow as large or as fast as female chickens. Consequently, hatcheries kill off their male chicks within hours of their birth, either suffocating them with gas or running them through a shredder to become animal feed.

2 Unsurprisingly, the death-by-grinder fate is a sticking point for animal rights activists and knowledgeable consumers alike. But what if the sex of a chicken could be determined while it was still an embryo? That's the question that has given rise to the world's first no-kill eggs, now being sold at a German grocery store chain, reports Josie Le Blond at *The Guardian*.

3 Ludger Breloh, managing director of egg technology company Seleggt, worked on a four-year program to find a more sustainable solution to the cull of male chicks for the grocery chain Rewe Group. To do so, he pulled on the research of Almuth Einspanier at the University of Leipzig, who's discovered a hormone present in female eggs that can be tested at nine days, well within the 21-day incubation period of an egg.

4 A Dutch company called HatchTech developed a way to mass test for the hormone estrone sulfate. The machine they came up with uses a laser to burn a tiny hole in an eggshell and then uses air pressure to push out a tiny drop of fluid for testing. The process takes approximately a second per egg, and allows male eggs to be pulled and disposed of before they hatch.

5 The no-kill eggs under the "Respeggt" brand that hit supermarkets in Berlin last month are from the first group of hens produced using this method. As production ramps up, the supermarket hopes to spread the brand to 5,500 other supermarkets in Germany next year.

Notes
egg and broiler industry 採卵養鶏産業
hatchery 孵化場
suffocate 窒息死させる run ~ through ... ～を（機械）にかける
sticking point 障害
animal rights activist 動物愛護運動家
embryo 胚
The Guardian ガーディアン紙（英国の新聞）
Seleggt ハッチテック社がレーベグループと共同で設立したジョイントベンチャー cull 間引き、間引きされた動物 Rewe Group ドイツの大手スーパー University of Leipzig ライプツィヒ大学 incubation period 孵化期間
HatchTech オランダの孵卵システムメーカー estrone sulfate 硫酸エストロン
hatch 孵化する
ramp up 増加する

6 According to a press release, Seleggt is currently developing a cost-neutral method to bring its technology to the poultry industry, and it hopes to have its sex-identification tech available to other hatcheries across Europe by 2020. But Breloh says determining the sex of the eggs is just a stop-gap solution. He says the bigger goal is to breed chickens in which both the females and males can be reared for market, eliminating the waste altogether.

7 Seleggt isn't the only company seeking solutions. Dan Charles at *NPR* reports that Austin-based egg producer Vital Farms has teamed up with the Israeli company Novatrans to analyze gases leaking through the pores of an egg to identify its sex after just two days of incubation. That tech has yet to make it to market. A researcher at McGill University in Montreal is also pursuing another method of sex identification that involves light.

8 Breloh tells Le Blond at *The Guardian* that he's happy other people are working on the problem. "Of course, there's competition, but it's positive in that it keeps us all focused on that goal," he says, which is ending chick culling for good.

Notes

cost-neutral
費用中立の（損をしない）
poultry 鶏肉

stop-gap 一時しのぎの

NPR
National Public Radio の略 (米国の非営利・公共のラジオネットワーク)
Vital Farms
米国で放牧卵を販売している会社
team up with ～
～と提携する
Novatrans
テルアビブのテクノロジー企業
pore 細孔
make it to ～ ～にたどり着く
McGill University
マギル大学

Comprehension Questions

A 記事の内容に一致するものには T（True）、一致しないものには F（False）を空所に書き入れましょう。

1. Male chicks aren't valuable to the egg and broiler industry despite their rapid growth rate. (　　)

2. A researcher at the University of Leipzig has discovered a hormone present in female eggs, and a Dutch company developed a mass test method for this hormone. (　　)

3. HatchTech developed a machine which uses a drill to make a small hole in an eggshell. (　　)

4. Seleggt is now developing a less expensive sex-identification method which can be employed by other hatcheries across Europe by 2020. (　　)

5. There may be other methods of determining the sex of the eggs; one involving light is now being studied. (　　)

B 以下は記事の要約です。適切な語を空所に書き入れ、音声を聞いて答えを確認しましょう。　　DL 14　　CD1-65

　　Currently (1. **m**　　　　　　) chicks are killed right after their birth by (2. **h**　　　　　　); either (3. **s**　　　　　) them or running them through a shredder to become animal (4. **f**　　　　　). To stop this (5. **c**　　　　　) culling, a more sustainable solution in which the (6. **s**　　　　　) of a chicken can be (7. **d**　　　　　) while it is still an (8. **e**　　　　　) has been found. In this method, estrone sulfate, a hormone present in (9. **f**　　　　　) eggs, is tested at nine days of (10. **i**　　　　　) and the process takes about a second per egg. The company is currently (11. **d**　　　　　) a cost-neutral method to spread this technology across Europe by 2020.

Read Better, Understand More!

動名詞・現在分詞

本文に登場した以下の文のように、科学記事では動詞に ing をつけた現在分詞や動名詞がしばしば使われます。

動名詞の例：

・Breloh says <u>determining</u> the sex of the eggs is just a stop-gap solution.
　determining の代わりに名詞 determination を使うと、この文は次のように変わります。
・Breloh says <u>the determination of</u> the sex of the eggs is just a stop-gap solution.
　動名詞というのは動詞から作られた名詞で、まだ動詞としての役割が残っているために直接目的語として the sex をとることができますが、動名詞ではない名詞 determination にはそのような働きがないため前置詞 of が必要になります。動名詞を使うことで of の繰り返しを避けることができ、文がすっきりするのです。

現在分詞の例：

・Seleggt isn't the only company <u>seeking</u> solutions.
　seeking は動詞 seek から派生した現在分詞で形容詞の働きをしています。seek を動詞のまま使うと、次のような関係代名詞 which が必要な複文構造になります。
・Seleggt isn't the only company <u>which seeks</u> solutions.

このように、動名詞や現在分詞を使用すると文の構造が簡単になり、また語数も減るというメリットがあるため、科学英語では好まれるのです。

Exercise　動名詞や現在分詞を使って文を簡潔にしましょう。

例：They analyze gases <u>which leak</u> through the pores of an egg.
　→　They analyze gases <u>leaking</u> through the pores of an egg.

1. The reliability of <u>the identification of</u> the human voice has been improved.
　→ _____

2. This publication introduces an analytical tool for <u>the study of</u> the properties.
　→ _____

3. Carrots are rich in β-carotene, <u>which helps</u> to maintain healthy eyes.
　→ _____

After You Read

A 会話を聞き、空所を埋めましょう。その後、会話をペアで練習しましょう。

🎧 DL 15 💿 CD1-66

David: Liz, you look so sad. What happened?

Liz: I just learned about chick culling. Did you know that [1.] _____ newborn male chicks in the USA every year?

David: Oh, I see. Don't be so pessimistic. Things are changing; they began to sell [2.] _____ .

Liz: Oh, really?

David: The scientists at the University of Leipzig have [3.] _____ , similar to a human pregnancy test, that can detect [4.] _____ .

Liz: That's great. The only concern is the [5.] _____ . I hope it won't be so expensive. I eat eggs every day, so it'll affect our family budget.

David: I'd buy no-kill eggs even if they were expensive. If many people start buying the eggs, the lives of many chickens will be saved in the future.

B あなた自身の意見を考え、クラスメートと話し合いましょう。

1. How do you find the culling of male chicks?
2. Would you buy no-kill eggs even though they were more expensive than ordinary eggs?

Behind the Scenes　オスのひよこの殺処分の現状と未来

日本でも、オスのひよこは生まれると殺処分されており、その数は年間1億羽にのぼります。殺処分の方法は、袋に入れて窒息、圧死、生きたまま機械で粉砕などです（参考：アニマルライツセンター公式サイト）。諸外国ではこの問題に関する意識が高く、ひよこが生まれる前にその雌雄を判別する方法に関しては、さまざまな研究が進められています。ドイツは世界に先駆けて「ノーキル」エッグを売り出しましたが、米国鶏卵生産者共同組合（United Egg Producers）も2020年までにオスのひよこの殺処分撤廃を目標にするとの声明を発表しています。

Unit 8

Why Scientists Want to Engineer Spicy Tomatoes

トマトとジャガイモが同時に実る「トムテト（TomTato)」は 2013 年に接ぎ木によって生まれました。その後、遺伝子工学により、味や日持ちのよいトマトが作り出されました。いま科学者たちはピリ辛トマトを作り出そうと研究しています。さて、なぜトマトを辛くしたいのでしょうか？

Before You Read

A 日本語の意味に合うように、空所に適切な語を語群から選んで書きましょう。語群には 1 つ余分なものがあります。

1. トマトの遺伝子を操作する　　　　　　genetically (　　　　　　　) tomatoes
2. 唐辛子と近縁関係にある　　　　　　　be closely (　　　　　　　) to peppers
3. 1900 万年前に分岐する　　　　　　　(　　　　　　　) 19 million years ago
4. ゲノムの特定領域を標的にする　　　　(　　　　　　　) specific regions of the genome
5. 唐辛子の白い内果皮の中に生じる
   (　　　　　　　) in the white pith of chilli peppers

describe	related	diverge	originate	target	engineer

B 下線部の英語の意味として適切な日本語を空所に書きましょう。

1. <u>genes</u> to produce capsaicinoids
   カプサイシノイド類を作り出すための（　　　　　　　　）
2. kick tomatoes' <u>capsaicin-producing</u> abilities into high gear
   トマトの（　　　　　　　　）能力を非常に高める
3. <u>vary</u> widely based on the environments
   環境によって大きく（　　　　　　　）
4. <u>affect</u> factors like crop yield and quality
   作物の収量や質といった因子に（　　　　　　　）
5. even with those <u>obstacles</u> in mind　　これらの（　　　　　　　）を考慮しても

Notes

1　If you were asked to describe a tomato, words like "juicy," "acidic" and maybe even "sweet" might pop into your mind. "Spicy" is not on the list of adjectives commonly attributed to this yummy fruit (and yes, it is a fruit), but that may one day change. As Nathaniel Scharping reports for *Discover*, a team of scientists hopes to genetically engineer tomatoes with a fiery kick.

2　The key to this challenge is capsaicin, the chemical compound that gives peppers their spicy taste by activating nerve cells in the tongue that deal with heat-induced pain. Because tomatoes are closely related to peppers—the two plants diverged 19 million years ago—they have all the genes necessary to produce capsaicinoids. But in tomatoes, these genes "are just not active," Agustin Zsögön, co-author of a new report published in *Trends in Plant Science*, tells *The Guardian's* Nicola Davis.

3　According to the paper, there are two ways that scientists can kick tomatoes' capsaicin-producing abilities into high gear. One is through CRISPR, the gene-editing tool that can target DNA at precise locations. The other option involves Transcription Activator-Like Effector Nucleases (TALENs), which similarly target specific regions of the genome and have in the past been used to alter the genes of several plant species.

4　All of this, of course, begs the question: Why are scientists so keen to infuse tomatoes with a bit of spicy punch? In the past, researchers have mulled over possible ways to create better-tasting tomatoes, but the team behind the new study is not overly concerned with starting a new culinary trend. Instead, the researchers hope to make it easier to harvest capsaicin's beneficial effects; the molecule has been shown to have anti-inflammatory, anti-oxidant and weight-loss properties. Capsaicin may even be helpful in fighting

acidic 酸っぱい

Discover
ディスカバー誌（米国のサイエンス誌）
a fiery kick
火を吹くほどスパイシーな味

capsaicinoid
カプサイシノイド

Trends in Plant Science
学術出版のエルゼビア社が発行しているジャーナル
The Guardian
ガーディアン紙（英国の新聞）
the paper　この論文

CRISPR　クリスパー
(Clustered Regularly Interspaced Short Palindromic Repeats の略)
TALEN
転写活性化因子様エフェクターヌクレアーゼ

beg the question
疑問を投げ掛ける
infuse　～を満たす
spicy punch
スパイシーな刺激
mull over ～
～について検討する

culinary　料理の

anti-inflammatory
抗炎症性の
anti-oxidant　抗酸化性の

cancer. On top of that, Zsögön tells Davis, capsaicinoids "are
used in [the] weapons industry for pepper spray [and] they
are also used for anaesthetics."

5 Capsaicinoids originate in the white pith of chilli peppers, which, unfortunately, are a rather finicky crop. They're
grown in open fields, leaving them susceptible to detrimental conditions like high precipitation and high tempera-
tures, and their capsaicinoid levels can vary widely based
on the environments in which they are cultivated. Peppers
are also vulnerable to soil-borne diseases, and their seed
germination can be quite slow. Contrast this with the hardy
tomato, which is often grown indoors, has a high yield and
is generally much easier to cultivate. Tomatoes, in other
words, may offer a promising avenue for producing capsaicinoids at a commercial level.

6 Granted, we haven't quite reached the point where
chefs will no longer have to add extra heat to their tomato
sauce. "We have the tools powerful enough to engineer the
genome of any species," notes Zsögön. "[T]he challenge is to
know which gene to engineer and where." Nor can scientists
be sure how tinkering with tomato genes will affect factors
like crop yield and quality. But even with those obstacles
in mind, the study authors are optimistic. Spicy tomatoes,
they write, could very well be "the next step in the fascinat-
ing story of pungent crops."

Notes

pepper spray
唐辛子スプレー、催涙スプレー
anaesthetic 麻酔薬

pith 内果皮

finicky 細心の注意を要する

susceptible to ~
～の影響を受けやすい
detrimental 有害な
precipitation 降水（量）
level 含有量

germination 発芽
hardy 頑丈な
yield 収穫量

promising avenue
有望な手段

tinker いじくり回す

pungent ピリっとする

Comprehension Questions

A 記事の内容に一致するものには T（True）、一致しないものには F（False）を空所に書き入れましょう。

1. A tomato is a delicious vegetable and can be described with such adjectives as "juicy," "acidic" and "sweet." （　　）

2. Scientists want to produce spicy tomatoes so that chefs will no longer need to add peppers to their tomato sauce. （　　）

3. Capsaicin contained in peppers has anti-inflammatory, anti-oxidant and weight-loss properties. （　　）

4. Currently capsaicinoids are obtained from chilli peppers which are not an ideal crop for producing capsaicinoids partly due to their unsteady capsaicinoid levels. （　　）

5. Scientists are confident that tinkering with tomato genes will not influence factors like crop yield and quality in a negative way. （　　）

B 以下は記事の要約です。適切な語を空所に書き入れ、音声を聞いて答えを確認しましょう。　　🎧 DL 16　　◎ CD1-73

Capsaicin is a (¹· c　　　　　) compound which gives peppers their (²· s　　　　　) taste, and has a lot of (³· b　　　　　) effects. Since tomatoes are closely related to peppers, they have all the (⁴· g　　　　　) necessary to produce capsaicinoids, but these genes are not (⁵· a　　　　　) in tomatoes. Scientists hope to activate these genes by (⁶· g　　　　　) engineering through CRISPR or TALENs. Peppers, grown in (⁷· o　　　　　) fields, are susceptible to harmful (⁸· c　　　　　) like a lot of rain and hot weather, and get (⁹· s　　　　　) diseases more easily. On the other hand, tomatoes are often grown (¹⁰· i　　　　　) and much easier to (¹¹· c　　　　　). Scientists hope that tomatoes will produce capsaicinoids at a (¹²· c　　　　　) level in the future.

Read Better, Understand More!

複合形容詞

本文に登場する以下の語句のように、複数の語をハイフンでつなげた複合形容詞は科学のニュースや記事でよく使われます。

heat-induced pain	熱［辛さ］誘発痛	（名詞＋過去分詞）
capsaicin-producing abilities	カプサイシン産生能力	（名詞＋現在分詞）
gene-editing tool	遺伝子編集ツール	（名詞＋現在分詞）
better-tasting tomatoes	よりおいしいトマト	（形容詞＋現在分詞）
soil-borne diseases	土壌伝染病	（名詞＋過去分詞）

複合形容詞のメリットは、語数が減ってスッキリまとまることです。
例えば heat-induced (pain) という複合形容詞は、名詞句では3語で表現され (pain which is) induced by heat「熱［辛さ］により誘発される（痛み）」となります。
また、複合形容詞の特徴として英語と日本語の語順が同じになることが挙げられます。

注意すべき点は、複合形容詞では複数名詞が単数名詞になることです。
例えば、「遺伝子を編集するツール」という名詞句では tool for editing genes と genes は複数ですが、複合形容詞では s が取れて gene-editing tool となります。

Exercise 次に示す名詞句から複合形容詞を作りましょう。

例：foods which are free from additives　→　additive-free foods
1. a necklace which is plated with gold　→　(　　　　　　　　　　　　　　　)
2. water which contains hydrogen　→　(　　　　　　　　　　　　　　　)
3. investigation that consumes money　→　(　　　　　　　　　　　　　　　)

After You Read

A 会話を聞き、空所を埋めましょう。その後、会話をペアで練習しましょう。

🎧 DL 17　　💿 CD1-74

Paul: Jane, have you ever heard of capsaicin?

Jane: Yes. Actually, I'm now taking ¹·＿＿＿＿＿＿＿＿＿＿＿＿＿＿＿＿＿＿
＿＿＿＿＿＿＿＿＿＿＿＿＿＿.

Paul: I see. Then, do you know that scientists are now trying to engineer spicy tomatoes containing capsaicin?

Jane: No, it's totally new to me. How come they want spicy tomatoes?

Paul: They let the hardy tomato produce capsaicin ²·＿＿＿＿＿＿＿＿＿＿＿
＿＿＿＿＿＿＿＿＿＿＿.

Jane: That's a good idea. If tomatoes can ³·＿＿＿＿＿＿＿＿＿＿＿＿＿＿＿＿
＿＿＿＿＿＿, my supplement may become cheaper.

Paul: Not only plants but also ⁴·＿＿＿＿＿＿＿＿＿＿＿＿＿＿＿＿＿
can produce beneficial medicines. For example, we now have a chicken which can produce an orphan drug* in its eggs.

Jane: That's great news for us. But I wonder if the ⁵·＿＿＿＿＿＿＿＿＿＿
＿＿＿＿＿＿＿＿＿＿＿＿＿ the chickens.

*orphan drug：希少疾病用医薬品。特定疾患などの薬物療法で、必要性が高いにもかかわらず患者数が少ないため製薬会社の採算が取れず、政府の援助などがないと製造されにくい処方箋医薬品。

B あなた自身の意見を考え、クラスメートと話し合いましょう。

1. If spicy tomatoes are on the market in the future, would you buy them? In other words, do you eat genetically modified foods?

2. Do you agree or disagree to using genetically modified animals for producing medicines?

Behind the Scenes　遺伝子組み替え技術の未来

2015 年、米国政府はライソゾーム酸性リパーゼ欠損症（LAL-D）の治療に使用される薬効成分を卵白内に生産する遺伝子組み換えニワトリを承認しました。ライソゾーム酸性リパーゼ欠損症は非常にまれな遺伝的疾患で、死亡リスクが高いものの、これまでは対症療法のみで、根本的な治療法がありませんでした。遺伝子組み換えニワトリから得られた薬は、LAL-D の根本的な原因に対処する唯一の承認薬で、日本では 2015 年 10 月に希少疾病用医薬品に指定されています。

Unit 9

Children Are Susceptible to Robot Peer Pressure

周囲の人の意見が全て「A」であるとき、自分だけ「B」とは言いにくい。本当は違う考えを持っていても、周りの人に合わせてしまうことを同調行動と呼びます。では、周りにいるのが人間ではなくロボットだったらどうでしょうか。子供たちを対象にした実験の結果は大人のものとは異なっていました。

Before You Read

A 日本語の意味に合うように、空所に適切な語を語群から選んで書きましょう。語群には１つ余分なものがあります。

1. 一致するものを見つけるよう求められる
   be asked to identify (　　　　　　) objects
2. 実験に参加する子供たちを募集する
   recruit children to (　　　　　　) in the experiment
3. 視力検査に見せかけた社会的同調試験
   a social (　　　　　　) test masquerading as a vision exam
4. 影響を及ぼすに十分な存在感　　　　enough presence to be (　　　　　　)
5. 子供よりも影響を受けにくい　　　　less (　　　　　) than children

matching conformity influential susceptible participate awareness

B 下線部の英語の意味として適切な日本語を空所に書きましょう。

1. the experiment was first <u>developed</u> during the 1950s
   この実験は最初 1950 年代に (　　　　　　) された
2. <u>wildly</u> varying lengths　　　　　長さが (　　　　　　) 異なる
3. the lines requiring assessment <u>remained</u> highly distinguishable
   判断を求められる線は、とても区別しやすい (　　　　　　)
4. humans <u>place faith</u> in machines　　人は機械を (　　　　　)
5. they <u>stuck</u> with their answers　　　彼らは自らの答えに (　　　　　　)

55

Reading

CD1-75 ～ CD1-86

Notes

1 It sounds like a plot from *Black Mirror*: Students are asked to identify matching objects, but when a robot chimes in with an obviously wrong answer, some kids repeat what the bot says verbatim instead of tapping into their own
5 smarts. But this isn't science fiction—a new study published in *Science Robotics* suggests kids easily succumb to peer pressure from robots.

2 *Discover*'s Bill Andrews reports that a team of German and British researchers recruited 43 children aged
10 between 7 and 9 to participate in the Asch experiment, a social conformity test masquerading as a vision exam. The experiment, which was first developed during the 1950s, asks participants to compare four lines and identify the two matching in length. There is an obviously correct answer, as
15 the lines are typically of wildly varying lengths, and when the children were tested individually, they provided the right response 87 percent of the time.

3 Once robots arrived on the scene, however, scores dropped to 75 percent.

20 **4** "When the kids were alone in the room, they were quite good at the task, but when the robots took part and gave wrong answers, they just followed the robots," study co-author Tony Belpaeme, a roboticist at the University of Plymouth in the United Kingdom, tells *The Verge*'s James
25 Vincent.

5 In the new testing environment, one volunteer at a time was seated alongside three humanoid robots. Although the lines requiring assessment remained highly distinguishable, child participants doubted themselves
30 and looked to their robot counterparts for guidance. Of the incorrect answers that the children provided, 74 percent matched those provided by the robots word for word.

6 Alan Wagner, an aerospace engineer at Pennsylvania

Black Mirror
Netflixが配信している近未来を舞台にしたSFドラマ
chime in 口をはさむ

bot ロボット
verbatim
一言一句そのままに
tap into ~ ～を利用する
Science Robotics
アメリカ科学振興協会（AAAS）が発行している、ロボティクスに関する論文を集めた雑誌
succumb 屈する
Discover
ディスカバー誌（米国のサイエンス誌）

masquerade 見せかける
vision exam 視力検査

participant 参加者

roboticist ロボット研究者
University of Plymouth
プリマス大学
The Verge
米国の技術系ニュースサイト

distinguishable 区別できる

counterpart 同等のもの［人］

word for word
一字一句違わずに
aerospace 航空宇宙の

56

State University who was not involved in the new study,
35 tells *The Washington Post*'s Carolyn Y. Johnson that the implacable faith humans often place in machines is known as "automation bias."

7 "People tend to believe these machines know more than they do, have greater awareness than they actually
40 do," Wagner notes. "They imbue them with all these amazing and fanciful properties."

8 *The Verge*'s Vincent writes that the researchers conducted the same test on a group of 60 adults. Unlike the children, these older participants stuck with their answers,
45 refusing to follow in the robots' (incorrect) footsteps.

9 The robots' demure appearance may have influenced adult participants' lack of faith in them, Belpaeme explains.

10 "[They] don't have enough presence to be influential," he tells Vincent. "They're too small, too toylike."

50 **11** Participants questioned at the conclusion of the exam verified the researchers' theory, stating that they assumed the robots were malfunctioning or not advanced enough to provide the correct answer. It's possible, Belpaeme notes, that if the study were repeated with more authoritative-
55 looking robots, adults would prove just as susceptible as children.

12 According to a press release, the team's findings have far-reaching implications for the future of the robotics industry. As "autonomous social robots" become increasingly
60 common in the education and child counseling fields, the researchers warn that protective measures should be taken to "minimize the risk to children during social child-robot interaction."

Notes

Pennsylvania State University
ペンシルバニア州立大学
The Washington Post
ワシントンポスト紙（米国の新聞）
implacable　執念深い

imbue ~ with ...
〜に…が備わっていると思う
fanciful　架空の、空想上の

follow in *one's* footsteps
（人）の先例にならう
demure　控えめな

malfunction
正常に機能しない

authoritative　権威ある

far-reaching　広範囲におよぶ

autonomous　自律型

Extra Notes

peer pressure：同調圧力。集団において、少数意見をもつ者に対し多数意見に合わせ行動するように暗黙のうちに強制すること。　**Asch experiment**：アッシュの同調実験。社会心理学者のソロモン・アッシュは、周囲の人々が不正解を選択すると、それに同調して自分も不正解を選択する人間の傾向（同調行動）を実験によって検証した。　**automation bias**：自動化バイアス。自動化意思決定システム（automated decision-making system）からの提案を好み、それに反する情報を、たとえそちらが正しくとも、無視する人間の傾向。　**social robot**：ソーシャルロボット。人間とのコミュニケーションを主眼においた、人間をサポートするロボット。コミュニケーションロボットやパーソナルロボットと呼ばれるもの。

Comprehension Questions

A 記事の内容に一致するものには T（True）、一致しないものには F（False）を空所に書き入れましょう。

1. German and British researchers recruited 43 teenagers for a social conformity test which is called the Asch experiment. （　　）
2. As the lines used in the Asch experiment are of similar length, participants have a hard time identifying the two matching in length. （　　）
3. When children were tested individually, they could give correct answers nearly 90% of the time; however, their scores dropped when robots were introduced and gave wrong answers. （　　）
4. The same experiment was repeated on a group of adult participants, and the result was similar to that of children. （　　）
5. In the test conducted on adult participants, the appearance of the robot may have influenced the result. （　　）

B 以下は記事の要約です。適切な語を空所に書き入れ、音声を聞いて答えを確認しましょう。　　🎧 DL 18　💿 CD1-87

According to a new study (1. p　　　　　　) in *Science Robotics*, kids easily (2. s　　　　　　) to peer pressure from robots. In this research 43 children (3. a　　　　　) between 7 and 9 (4. p　　　　　　) in the Asch (5. e　　　　　), which asks participants to (6. c　　　　　) four lines and identify the two matching in (7. l　　　　　). When the children were tested (8. i　　　　　), they were quite (9. g　　　　) at the task and provided the right response 87 percent of the time. But when the robots took (10. p　　　　　) and gave wrong answers, children just followed the robots and scores dropped to 75 percent. The results suggest that protective measures should be taken to "minimize the risk to children during social child-robot (11. i　　　　　)."

Read Better, Understand More!

複合名詞　1

複合名詞とは簡単に言うと、名詞をいくつか並べて作る新しい名詞のことです。同じ内容を少ない語数で簡潔に表現できるため、科学分野の文章で多用されています。この Unit では robot peer pressure という複合名詞が登場しました。これは名詞句にすると peer pressure from robots となりますが、よく見るとこの peer pressure も実は複合名詞で、pressure from peers と書き換えることができるのです。

さて、複合名詞は英文を書くときにますます威力を発揮します。名詞と名詞の組み合わせで作るのですが、名詞句と異なり、それぞれの名詞の前に冠詞や前置詞が不要になるからです。重要なのは名詞を並べる順番です。それでは、複合名詞を作る手順を確認しましょう。

a system for the purification of water「水を浄化するためのシステム」という名詞句を複合名詞に変えてみます。

手順 1)　名詞句の先頭にある名詞（ここでは system）を複合名詞の末尾に持ってきます。
手順 2)　残りの名詞（ここでは purification と water）が複数形の場合は単数形に直してから、元とは逆の語順に並べます。
手順 3)　名詞句の先頭の名詞の冠詞がそのまま複合名詞の冠詞として使われます。

ところで、日本語にも複合名詞は存在します。上記の「水を浄化するためのシステム」の複合名詞は「水浄化システム」で、英語の a water purification system と全く同じ語順になります。Unit 8 の複合形容詞の場合と同様ですね。

Exercise　次に示す名詞句から複合名詞を作りましょう。

1. an analysis carried out using X-ray　→　an (　　　　　　) (　　　　　　)
2. a wire made of copper　　　　　　　→　a (　　　　　　) (　　　　　　)
3. the consumption of fossil fuels
　→　the (　　　　　) (　　　　　) (　　　　　)

After You Read

A 会話を聞き、空所を埋めましょう。その後、会話をペアで練習しましょう。

🎧 DL 19　　◎ CD1-88

Alex: Grace, have you ever heard the expression "KY"?

Grace: KY? What does it mean?

Alex: KY, or "Kuki ga Yomenai," is 1.＿＿＿＿＿＿＿＿＿＿＿＿＿＿＿＿＿＿
＿＿＿＿＿＿＿＿＿. It can be literally translated as 2. "＿＿＿＿＿＿＿＿＿＿
＿＿＿＿＿＿＿＿＿＿＿＿＿." In some situations, this expression is similar to
3. "＿＿＿＿＿＿＿＿＿＿＿＿＿＿＿＿＿＿＿＿＿＿＿" in English.

Grace: I see. I feel that in Japan, conformity is very highly regarded. People often
4.＿＿＿＿＿＿＿＿＿＿＿＿＿＿＿＿＿＿＿＿＿＿＿ rather than to pursue
personal desires.

Alex: You are wrong. Conformity is everywhere. As shown in the Asch experiment originally conducted in the USA, if all the surrounding people choose
a wrong answer, 5.＿＿＿＿＿＿＿＿＿＿＿＿＿＿＿＿＿＿＿＿＿＿＿ and
choose the wrong answer, even though he knows it's wrong.

B あなた自身の意見を考え、クラスメートと話し合いましょう。

1. If you participated in the Asch experiment using robots, do you think wrong
   answers from them would have any influence on your response?
2. What are the merits and demerits of conformity?

Behind the Scenes　アッシュの同調実験

1951 年に心理学者のソロモン・アッシュが行った同調実験とは、2 枚のカード A、B を
用意し、A には 1 本の線分を、B には長さの異なる 3 本の線分を描き、被験者に長さの
等しい線分を選ばせるというものでした。3 本の線分の長さは明らかに異なっており、
正しい答えを選択するのは困難ではありません。8 名の被験者の内、7 名はサクラで、
彼らは初めの 2、3 回は正しい答えを選択するものの、その後は全員揃って間違った答
えを選択する手はずになっています。真の被験者はサクラたちが答えた後で答えます。
サクラ全員が正解を答えると、被験者も堂々と正しい選択肢を選びましたが、サクラた
ちが不正解を答えると、真の被験者の 75％は最低 1 回、間違った答えを選択し、サクラ
たちに同調したのです。この実験により、問いに対する正解、不正解が明らかな場合でも、
周囲の人々が不正解を選択すると、それに同調して自分も不正解の答えを選んでしまう
という人間の傾向が証明されたのでした。

Unit 10

British Doctors May Soon Prescribe Art, Music, Dance, Singing Lessons

お医者さんからの処方箋を持って患者さんが訪れるのは美術館？　コンサート？　それとも舞踊教室？　芸術に触れることは肉体的、精神的な健康の改善に役立つという視点に立ち「社会的処方」とよばれる試みが始まっています。

Before You Read

A 日本語の意味に合うように、空所に適切な語を語群から選んで書きましょう。語群には１つ余分なものがあります。

1. 芸術に基づく治療法を処方する　（　　　　　　） therapeutic art-based treatments
2. 芸術と触れ合う　　　　　　　　（　　　　　　） with the arts
3. 精神病初期の兆候を示す　　　　display early（　　　　） of psychosis
4. 社会的処方はより伝統的な形の治療の代わりとしてではなく、それを補完するものとして想定されている
   social prescribing is intended to（　　　　　） rather than replace more traditional forms of treatment
5. 適切な財政支援を保証する　　　ensure（　　　　　） funding

> **adequate　prescribe　complement　signs　engage　strategy**

B 下線部の英語の意味として適切な日本語を空所に書きましょう。

1. an ambitious initiative　　（　　　　　　　　）構想
2. enroll in dance classes　　舞踊クラスに（　　　　　　）
3. encourage patients to play instruments
   楽器を演奏するよう患者に（　　　　　　）
4. pilot programs are already underway
   （　　　　　　） プログラムはすでに進行中である
5. value the arts　　　　　　芸術を（　　　　　　）

Reading

CD1-89 ～ CD1-95

Notes

British Health Secretary 英国保健相	

1 An ambitious initiative unveiled this week by British Health Secretary Matt Hancock may soon enable the country's doctors to prescribe therapeutic art- or hobby-based treatments for ailments ranging from dementia to psy-
5 chosis, lung conditions and mental health issues. Writing for the *Times*, Kat Lay explains that this unconventional strategy, described by the UK government as "social prescribing," could find patients enrolled in dance classes and singing lessons, or perhaps enjoying a personalized music
10 playlist.

2 The medical benefits of engaging with the arts are well-recorded: As Lay notes, a collaboration between the Royal Philharmonic Orchestra and stroke survivors living in Hull, England, encouraged patients to play instruments,
15 conduct and perform; 90 percent of these participants reported improvements in their physical and mental health. In Lambeth, dance lessons have been shown to improve concentration and communication skills amongst those displaying early signs of psychosis, and in Gloucestershire,
20 hospitals have begun to refer individuals with lung conditions to singing sessions.

3 A similar campaign launched in Canada earlier this month, Brendan Kelly reports for the *Montreal Gazette*. Beginning on November 1, every member of the Montreal-
25 based medical association Médecins francophones du Canada (MdFC) gained the option of handing out 50 prescriptions allowing patients and a limited number of friends, family and caregivers to tour Quebec's Montreal Museum of Fine Arts for free. Normally, admission costs up to $23 Ca-
30 nadian dollars (roughly $18 USD). As MdFC vice president Hélène Boyer tells Kelly, the initiative builds on research suggesting museum visits raise serotonin levels to offer a quick mood-boost.

therapeutic 治療の

ailment 病気
dementia 認知症
psychosis 精神病

Times
タイムズ紙（英国の新聞）
unconventional
型破りの

Royal Philharmonic
Orchestra
ロイヤルフィルハーモニー管弦
楽団
Hull ハル

Lambeth ランベス

amongst ～の間で

Gloucestershire
グロスターシャー州
refer ～ to ...
（患者）を（専門医など）に紹介
する

Montreal Gazette
モントリオールガゼット紙（カ
ナダのモントリオールで唯一英
語で発行されている日刊紙）
Médecins francophones
du Canada (MdFC)
カナダのフランス語圏の医師
（会）

caregiver 介護者
Montreal Museum of Fine
Arts
モントリオール美術館

build on ~
～に基づいてことを進める
serotonin level
セロトニン値（濃度）

62

4 Compared to the Canadian project, the UK one is si-
35 multaneously more comprehensive and less fleshed-out. Rather than simply prescribing one museum trip, the British campaign will encompass multiple walks of life, from social activities such as cooking classes, playing bingo and gardening to more culturally focused ventures, including
40 library visits and concerts.

5 Social prescribing is intended to complement rather than replace more traditional forms of treatment. As Sally Copley, director of policy for the Alzheimer's Society, explains, music and the arts must function in conjunction
45 with "access to the right support and medication when needed and, crucially, the government ensuring adequate funding for care is addressed."

6 According to *The Stage*'s Georgia Snow, pilot programs are already underway in England's northwest,
50 where there's a social prescribing scheme specifically for new mothers and babies, and in Wales, where the National Health Service has teamed up with the country's arts council.

7 "We should value the arts because they're essential to
55 our health and wellbeing," Hancock said in his remarks earlier this week. "Access to the arts improves people's mental and physical health. It makes us happier and healthier."

fleshed-out 具体化された

encompass 包含する
walk 分野

venture 冒険的試み

Alzheimer's Society
アルツハイマー協会
in conjunction with ~
~と共に、~と併せて

crucially 決定的に、重大に

The Stage
舞踊、オペラ、劇場情報などを
発信している英国の週刊誌、ウェ
ブサイト
underway 進行中で

National Health Service
国民医療保健サービス
team up with ~
~と協力する
arts council 芸術協議会

wellbeing 幸福

Comprehension Questions

A 記事の内容に一致するものには T（True）、一致しないものには F（False）を空所に書き入れましょう。

1. According to the ambitious initiative, British doctors will be able to prescribe therapeutic art- or hobby-based treatments specifically for mental illness.

   (　　　)

2. The unconventional strategy is described by the UK government as "social prescribing" and patients could be enrolled in dance classes, singing lessons, cooking classes, or gardening, etc.　(　　　)

3. In a collaboration between the Royal Philharmonic Orchestra and stroke survivors living in Hull, most of the patients reported improvements in their health.

   (　　　)

4. This ambitious initiative has no precedent and has been launched only in England.　(　　　)

5. According to Hancock, the arts are absolutely necessary for our health and well-being.　(　　　)

B 以下は記事の要約です。適切な語を空所に書き入れ、音声を聞いて答えを確認しましょう。　🎧 DL 20　💿 CD1-96

The UK government (¹· **u**　　　　) an ambitious (²· **i**　　　　) to allow the country's doctors to (³· **p**　　　　) therapeutic art- or hobby-based treatments for (⁴· **a**　　　　) ranging from (⁵· **d**　　　　) to (⁶· **p**　　　　), lung (⁷· **c**　　　　) and mental health issues. The medical benefits of engaging with the arts are well-known; as an example, a (⁸· **c**　　　　) between a famous orchestra and stroke (⁹· **s**　　　　) resulted in physical and mental health (¹⁰· **i**　　　　) in 90% of the participants. Social (¹¹· **p**　　　　), however, should not entirely replace conventional treatment.

Read Better, Understand More!

複合名詞　2

複合名詞についてさらに詳しくみていきましょう。本文に登場した複合名詞をリストアップします。

lung condition「肺疾患」、dance class「舞踊授業」、singing lesson「歌のレッスン」
stroke survivor「脳卒中生還患者」、communication skill「コミュニケーションスキル」、
museum visit「美術館訪問」、museum trip「美術館見学」、library visit「図書館訪問」

複合名詞は複数の名詞から構成されています。上記の singing lesson や Unit 7 に出てきた chick culling に見られるように動名詞が用いられることもあります。末尾に来る名詞（singing lesson の場合は lesson）がその複合名詞の本質を表す名詞です。その前に来る名詞（singing lesson の場合は singing）は情報を付け加える（修飾する）役割を持っているため、常に単数形の名詞が用いられます。

複合名詞には、前置詞 of の繰り返しを避けることができるという利点があります。日本語でも「ラットの肺の疾患」を「ラットの肺疾患」と複合名詞を利用して「の」の数を減らすことができますが、英語でも同様に a condition of a lung of a rat を a lung condition of a rat とすることで of の数を減らすことができるのです。

Exercise　複合名詞を利用して下記の名詞句から of を 1 つ（または 2 つ）減らしましょう。

例：a condition of a lung of a rat　→　a lung condition of a rat

1. the importance of the skill of communication
→　(　　　　　) (　　　　　) (　　　　　) (　　　　　) (　　　　　)

2. the visit of a museum of your choice
→　(　　　　　) (　　　　　) (　　　　　) (　　　　　) (　　　　　)
(　　　　　)

3. the principle of conservation of energy
→　(　　　　　) (　　　　　) (　　　　　) (　　　　　)

After You Read

A 会話を聞き、空所を埋めましょう。その後、会話をペアで練習しましょう。

🎧 DL 21   ⦿ CD1-97

Ava: I visited my grandmother yesterday. 1.

_____ , but it seems she's doing better these days.

Ethan: That's great. The medicine 2._____ ,

maybe.

Ava: Actually, she's now attending a drawing class. Her doctor has written

3._____ . She says she

enjoys it very much.

Ethan: Oh, I read an article about social prescribing in yesterday's newspaper.

Patients can 4._____ ranging

from art classes, gardening to gym exercises, right?

Ava: Yes. I think it puts less strain on our body than taking pills. It may not

5._____ , though.

B あなた自身の意見を考え、クラスメートと話し合いましょう。

1. Do you agree or disagree with social prescribing?
2. What are the merits and demerits of social prescribing in comparison with more traditional forms of treatment?

Behind the Scenes   社会的処方

「社会的処方：薬をのむより体を動かせ」というタイトルで英国の「社会的処方箋（social prescriptions）」についての紹介が NPO 法人アジア情報フォーラムのサイトに掲載されています。それによると、リバプールでは開業医からの依頼に基づいて患者にウクレレやタンゴ・ダンス、コーラスなどを教える教室が開かれており、従来の治療に比べ、コストは 10 分の 1 程度で済んでいるそうです。また、ロンドンではカーン市長の方針で、50 を越える社会的処方グループが活動しており、開業医に通う患者数が 28％減少、緊急治療室に送られてくる患者数も 24％減っているとのことです。

Unit 11

This Remote Control Vest Trains Rescue Dogs Using Flashlights

人とロボット技術と災害救助犬を融合した新しい被災者探索方法が開発されています。救助犬用の軽量ベストには懐中電灯が備わっていて、この光を利用し、犬をリモートコントロールするのです。被災地などの苛酷な現場での救助犬の活躍が一層期待できます。

Before You Read

A 日本語の意味に合うように、空所に適切な語を語群から選んで書きましょう。語群には１つ余分なものがあります。

1. 非常に有用な道具　　　　　　　　an (　　　　　　) useful tool
2. 実際にはこのベストで犬を導く　　in (　　　　　　), the vest guides the dogs
3. 基本的に、犬は両側に懐中電灯のついたベストを着用する
   (　　　　　　), the dog wears a vest with flashlights on either side
4. 光を遠隔操作する　　　　　　　　(　　　　　　) the lights from afar
5. 損傷したプラントの内部を調べる素晴らしい方法
   a great way to (　　　　　) inside the damaged plant

| reality | aim | incredibly | essentially | trap | look |

B 下線部の英語の意味として適切な日本語を空所に書きましょう。

1. a new vest allows dog <u>handlers</u> to control their puppers
   犬の (　　　　　　) は新しいベストを使って犬をコントロールできる
2. similar disaster <u>scenarios</u>　　　　類似した災害 (　　　　　)
3. an ability to <u>sniff out</u> victims　　被害者を (　　　　　) 能力
4. people are <u>invisible</u> in a vast area but in need of urgent help
   広大なエリアのどこかに (　　　　　) 緊急の援助が必要な人がいる
5. the system was successfully <u>tested</u>
   このシステムの (　　　　　) は成功した

Reading

CD2-01 ~ CD2-08

Notes

1 As K9 cops, search and rescue teams, and drug enforcement agents know, a well-trained dog is an incredibly useful tool—not to mention an excellent furry companion. But there are some situations where that relationship breaks
5 down, like in loud settings or when a dog has to travel into an area where it can't see or hear its handler. Now, a Japanese lab has come up with a new vest that allows dog handlers to control their puppers via "remote control."

K9
（canine の略で）警察犬
cop 警官
search and rescue
探索救助
drug enforcement
麻薬取り締まり
furry 毛皮で覆われた

lab
（laboratory の略で）研究所
pupper わんちゃん

2 In reality, the vest guides the dogs via flashlights, reports
10 Andrew Liszewski at *Gizmodo*. In a recently posted video, researchers from Tohoku University demonstrate the gadget. Essentially, the dog wears a vest with flashlights on either side. The lights can be aimed from afar, creating bright spots on the ground. The dog is then able to follow
15 the lights around obstacles, which, in the case of the lab demonstration, is a series of folding tables.

flashlight
懐中電灯
Gizmodo
最新テクノロジーに関する
ニュースを扱うテクノロジーメ
ディアサイト
gadget 装置

afar 遠くに

3 This is not the first time roboticist Kazunori Ohno and his team at Tohoku University have upgraded search and rescue (SAR) dogs. (No, we're not talking about robotic
20 dogs, like Sony's Aibo.) Mai Iida at *The Japan Times* reports that Ohno began working on a project called the Robo-Dog system in 2011, after helping with the remote-controlled robotic crawlers used during the Fukushima nuclear disaster.

roboticist ロボット研究者

robotic ロボットの

The Japan Times
ジャパンタイムズ紙（日本の英
字新聞）

robotic crawler
クローラーロボット
nuclear disaster
核（原子炉）による災害

4 While the robotic crawler was a great way to look
25 inside the damaged plant, Ohno realized that in many similar disaster scenarios there are people trapped inside but unable to communicate or make their presence known. In that case, a dog and its ability to sniff out victims are irreplaceable.

irreplaceable
他のものと置き換えられない
rescuer 救助者

5 "We often hear from rescuers that there are cases
30 where people are invisible in a vast area but in need of urgent help," says Ohno. "Dogs can find people with their strong olfactory sense. When exploring a new way to search,

olfactory sense 嗅覚

we came up with the idea of forming a tag team with dogs
35 (and robotic technology)."

6 That led to the development of a special cyber suit for rescue dogs two years ago that at the time only included GPS, motion tracking sensors and cameras, so rescuers could keep track of their dogs using a phone or iPad as
40 the pooches entered a search area. The equipment is light enough that the dogs can wear the vest for over an hour without getting fatigued.

7 In 2016, *Agence France Presse* reported the system was successfully tested with Robo-Dog equipped SAR animals
45 finding survivors in a mock earthquake drill, and the suit was then made available to SAR teams in Japan. The addition of the dog-directing spotlights, if and when they are perfected, will make the system even more useful.

8 Regardless, any hard-working, high-tech hound is a
50 very, very good doggo.

Notes

tag team
タッグチーム（共に仕事をする
2人（以上）の人）

cyber suit　サイバースーツ

motion tracking　動作追跡

pooch　犬

fatigued　疲れ切った

Agence France Presse
アジャンス・フランス・プレス
（AFP）。フランスの通信社。

mock　模擬の
drill　訓練、演習

hound　犬、猟犬

doggo　犬

Extra Note

handler：一般には犬の調教師などを指すが、ここでは犬に指示を与える人のこと

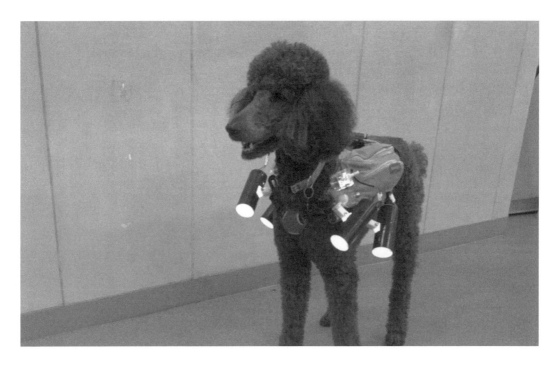

Comprehension Questions

A 記事の内容に一致するものには T（True）、一致しないものには F（False）を空所に書き入れましょう。

1. Well-trained dogs are very helpful in finding people at a disaster site even when they cannot hear or see their handler. （　　　）

2. A roboticist at Tohoku University had experience in working on the remote-controlled robotic crawlers before he started the Robo-dog project. （　　　）

3. Kazunori Ohno and his team were recommended to use real dogs instead of robotic technology. （　　　）

4. The special cyber suit for rescue dogs was initially developed two years ago but it did not allow the handler to control his dog. （　　　）

5. The cyber suit became available for SAR teams in Japan, only after the system was successfully tested with Robo-Dog equipped SAR animals. （　　　）

B 以下は記事の要約です。適切な語を空所に書き入れ、音声を聞いて答えを確認しましょう。　　　🎧 DL 22　　◎ CD2-09

Researchers at Tohoku University have come up with a new (¹· c　　　　　　) suit for (²· s　　　　　) and rescue (SAR) dogs. SAR dogs are very useful in many (³· d　　　　　) scenes for finding (⁴· s　　　　　). The old suit developed previously was equipped with GPS, motion tracking sensors and cameras, so (⁵· r　　　　　) could keep (⁶· t　　　　　) of their dogs using a phone or iPad as the pooches entered a search area. The new suit has two (⁷· f　　　　　) on either side and the dog wearing the suit is guided by the bright (⁸· s　　　　　) on the ground created by the flashlights which can be (⁹· a　　　　　) from afar.

Read Better, Understand More!

$$\boxed{\text{冠詞} \quad 1}$$

本文では「犬」を表す単語が 22 回登場します。「犬」を表す単語と言えば dog ですが、欧米のライターたちは同じ単語の繰り返しを嫌うため、ここでは dog の他に K9、pupper、pooch、hound、doggo が使用されています。

同じ単語の繰り返しを嫌うのは、読み物としての記事に限った話ではなく、論文などでも同じです。例えば、エチルアルコールを溶媒として使用している化学論文の中で、エチルアルコールは最初は ethyl alcohol「エチルアルコール」と紹介されますが、次からは the alcohol「（この）アルコール」、the solvent「（この）溶媒」などと言い換えられていきます。つまり、初めて出てきたにも関わらず alcohol に the がついていたら、それは前に出てきた ethyl alcohol を言い換えているのだと分かります。the ではなくて an alcohol と an がついていれば、それは具体的に何かは分からない「単なる一つのアルコール」を指していることになります。

Exercise 次の文は酸（acid、ここでは例として塩酸（HCl）を使用）と塩基（base、ここでは水酸化ナトリウム（NaOH）を使用）を混合した時に生じる中和反応（neutralization reaction）について記載したものです。空欄に適切な冠詞（a/an、または the）を書き入れましょう。

When hydrochloric acid (HCl) and sodium hydroxide (NaOH) are mixed, a neutralization reaction occurs, and you will get sodium chloride (NaCl) and water. Here, (1.＿＿＿＿＿＿) salt is the product between (2.＿＿＿＿＿＿) base and (3.＿＿＿＿＿＿) acid.

After You Read

会話を聞き、空所を埋めましょう。その後、会話をペアで練習しましょう。

🎧 DL 23　　💿 CD2-10

Josh: Kate, look at this beautiful girl on my iPad screen! Her name is Erica and she is said to be ¹. _____ human-oid robot.

Kate: Gee, she looks so real!

Josh: They say "Japan is the land of rising robotics*." ². _____ _____ like Human Robots, Androids, and Animal Robots.

Kate: I heard during the Fukushima nuclear disaster, ³. _____ _____ were deployed to examine the damaged plant.

Josh: Robots can do things ⁴. _____, but they are not almighty. To find survivors buried in collapsed buildings** etc., SAR dogs are really useful.

Kate: That's why they came up with a cyber suit for SAR dogs. ⁵. _____ _____ is formed of a researcher, a dog and robotic technology!

*robotics：ロボット工学
**collapsed building：倒壊した建物

あなた自身の意見を考え、クラスメートと話し合いましょう。

1. What do you think of the idea of developing a cyber suit for a rescue dog?
2. Can you think of other animals which can be used to rescue people? How can they help us? Can you imagine any special cyber suit for them?

Behind the Scenes　災害時に活躍するロボット

生存者を探しだす点でSAR犬の役割は大きいですが、人や動物の命が危険にさらされる環境ではタフなロボットが大活躍します。例えば、クローラー型ロボットは災害で閉鎖した地下街や半倒壊した建物を探査するために開発された、全身が移動用のクローラベルトで覆われ、腕のように稼働する4本のクローラベルトをそなえた平たいロボットです。階段や起伏の激しい場所の移動も可能で、カメラなどの搭載機器により現場の情報収集を行います。また、ドローンを利用した飛行ロボットも開発されています。飛行中に何かにぶつかっても落下しないように、全身が透明な丸い殻（かご）に覆われており、地上移動ロボットがアクセスできない場所に飛んで行き、その場の状況を撮影して送信するのです。

Unit 12

Sans Forgetica Is the Typeface You Won't Forget

キャラ（性格）に特徴がある人は、ない人よりも記憶に残るようです。ならば、文字（character）の一部を消して、隙間だらけの不完全な文字を作れば、その文字で書かれた内容は私たちの記憶によりしっかりと残るのでしょうか。認知心理学の「望ましい困難」と呼ばれる原理に基づいて画期的なフォントが作り出されました。

The font to remember
RMIT UNIVERSITY

Before You Read

A 日本語の意味に合うように、空所に適切な語を語群から選んで書きましょう。語群には１つ余分なものがあります。

1. 試験のために詰め込み勉強をする （　　　　　　　　） for exams
2. 思考の交流が新しいフォントの誕生につながった
　（　　　　　　　　） of thinking has led to the creation of a new font
3. 標準の読み取り方［パターン］を覆す
　（　　　　　　　　） conventional reading patterns
4. 「望ましい困難」という心理学の原理に従う
　（　　　　　　　　） to the psychological principle of "desirable difficulty"
5. このフォントを広く採用する （　　　　　　　　） this font universally

> **cross-pollination　cram　subvert　adhere　highlight　adopt**

B 下線部の英語の意味として適切な日本語を空所に書きましょう。

1. character flaws can make a person <u>all the more</u> memorable
　性格の欠陥により、その人が（　　　　　　　　）記憶に残ることがある
2. <u>retain</u> more information　　　より多くの情報を（　　　　　　）
3. the font also <u>back-slants</u>　　　さらにこのフォントは（　　　　　　　）
4. take these <u>attributes</u> at type-face value
　これらの（　　　　　　　　）を鵜呑みにする
5. <u>bring on</u> a migraine　　　片頭痛を（　　　　　　）

Reading

CD2-11 ~ CD2-19

Notes

1 Sometimes, character flaws can make a person—or a thing—all the more memorable. Such may be the case with Sans Forgetica, a new gap-ridden typeface released (for free) last week by researchers at RMIT University in Melbourne, Australia.

2 According to an RMIT press release, this font is the first specifically designed to help its readers retain more information—a potential perk for students cramming for exams, for instance. The typeface was born out of a multidisciplinary research effort that combined the skill sets of design specialists, psychologists and more.

3 "This cross-pollination of thinking has led to the creation of a new font that is fundamentally different from all [others]," Stephen Banham, a typography expert at RMIT, says in the press release.

4 And Sans Forgetica—with its cheeky, literal name—is indeed pretty memorable. Entire hunks of each character are left off the page, giving them a slightly disjointed or haphazard appearance. The font also back-slants, or leans to the left (the opposite direction of *italics*, which tilt rightward)—something typically used only in cartography when indicating rivers, reports Taylor Telford at *The Washington Post*.

5 These unique characteristics, which fly in the face of conventional text, make readers think twice about what's in front of them. "We've actually subverted … conventional reading patterns," explains Banham, in an interview with Scott Simon at *NPR*.

6 Such a meticulous strategy adheres to the psychological principle of "desirable difficulty," increasing the effort that readers have to put into understanding text, which helps solidify the material at hand in memory, according to the RMIT press release. For instance, to fill in the gaps in

Notes
flaw 欠陥
gap-ridden すきまだらけの typeface 書体 RMIT University Royal Melbourne Institute of Technology 大学。オーストラリアのメルボルンに本部を置く国立大学。
perk (perquisite の略で) 恩恵 multidisciplinary 多くの専門分野にわたる、学際的な
typography タイポグラフィー（書体の選択、配列など）
cheeky ずうずうしい literal 文字通りの hunk （大きな）塊
disjointed ばらばらの
haphazard 無計画な
tilt 傾く rightward 右側に cartography 地図製作
The Washington Post ワシントンポスト紙（米国の新聞）
fly in the face of ~ （慣例など）を無視して行動する think twice 熟考する
NPR National Public Radio の略（米国の非営利・公共のラジオネットワーク） meticulous 細部に気を配った desirable difficulty 望ましい困難 solidify 固める

each character, the brain is forced to pause and puzzle out
35 the pieces.

| 7   But the team didn't just take these attributes at type-
face value. Recruiting about 400 Australian students, they
conducted an online experiment to test the memory-boosting power of several different fonts. When participants read
40 text in plain Arial, they remembered about half of it. But
Sans Forgetica readers recalled about 57 percent of their
material, *The Guardian* reports.

| 8   As for adopting Sans Forgetica universally? Forget
about it. As Banham tells Simon, reading a novel in Sans
45 Forgetica would be an efficient way to bring on a migraine.

| 9   Instead, Banham sees his typeface as a tool for the stu-
dious to highlight specific passages or key phrases, only in
a "very, very selective manner," he says to Simon. According
to *The Guardian*, Janneke Blijlevens of RMIT's Behavioral
50 Business Lab adds foreign language learners and elderly
people grappling with memory loss to the list of potential
beneficiaries.

Notes

memory-boosting
記憶を促進する

Arial　欧文用フォントの一つ

The Guardian
ガーディアン紙（英国の新聞）
universally　広く

migraine　片頭痛

studious　学問に励む

RMIT's Behavioral
Business Lab
RMIT大学の研究所。ビジネス上
の意思決定を心理学的アプロー
チにより研究している。
grapple with ~
～と格闘する
beneficiary　恩恵を受ける人

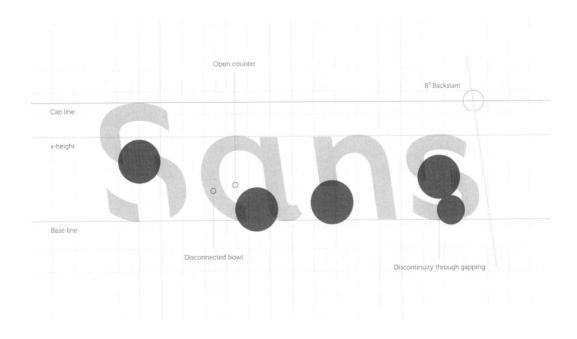

Comprehension Questions

A 記事の内容に一致するものには T （True）、一致しないものには F （False） を空所に書き入れましょう。

1. Sans Forgetica is a relatively inexpensive uniquely designed typeface produced and released by researchers at RMIT University. （   ）

2. The font was originally designed to help its readers keep more information, but it turned out to be the cause of migraines. （   ）

3. Design specialists, psychologists and other professionals worked together to create the typeface. （   ）

4. Sans Forgetica, having a slightly disjointed or haphazard appearance, is pretty memorable. （   ）

5. The memory-boosting power of Sans Forgetica was proved by an online experiment conducted with 400 Australian students. （   ）

B 以下は記事の要約です。適切な語を空所に書き入れ、音声を聞いて答えを確認しましょう。　　　　　　　　　　　　　　　　🎧 DL 24　　💿 CD2-20

　　Sans Forgetica is the first (¹· **s**　　　　　　) designed (²· **f**　　　　　　) to help its readers retain more information. The typeface resulted from a (³· **m**　　　　　　) research effort that involved (⁴· **d**　　　　　　) specialists, (⁵· **p**　　　　　　) and more. This new (⁶· **g**　　　　　　) typeface (⁷· **l**　　　　　　) to the left [the opposite direction of (⁸· **i**　　　　　　), which tilt (⁹· **r**　　　　　　)].

　　The design of the font is based on the (¹⁰· **p**　　　　　　) principle of "(¹¹· **d**　　　　　　) (¹²· **d**　　　　　　)." This font can be useful for students (¹³· **c**　　　　　　) for exams, foreign language (¹⁴· **l**　　　　　　), and elderly people suffering from (¹⁵· **m**　　　　　　) loss.

Read Better, Understand More!

冠詞　2

英語には日本語に存在しない「冠詞」というものがありますが、みなさんはあまり冠詞には注意を払っていないのではないでしょうか。冠詞なんか無視しても意味はとれると思うべからず。冠詞は実はとても重要な働きをしているのです。a と表すべきところを the にしたり、その逆を行うと、英文の意味が大きく変わってしまうこともあります。では、英語の a と the について、本文の 7 段落目の文を例に少し詳しく見て行きましょう。

But the team didn't just take these attributes at type-face value. Recruiting about 400 Australian students, they conducted an online experiment ...
ここで the を a に、an を the に変えてみると、意味はどう変わるでしょうか。
But a team didn't just take these attributes at type-face value. Recruiting about 400 Australian students, they conducted the online experiment ...

まず、the team であれば、RMIT 大学で本研究に携わっている研究者たちを指しているので、訳文は「しかし、彼らはこれらの特徴を鵜呑みにしなかった」となります。一方で、a team は「ある一つのチーム」という意味しかないので、訳文は「しかし、あるチームはこれらの特徴を鵜呑みにしなかった」となります。特徴を鵜呑みにしなかったチームと鵜呑みにしたチームが存在することをほのめかしている文章になってしまいます。

次の they conducted an online experiment は、オンライン実験を行った、という意味ですが、the online experiment とすると、すでにオンライン実験の話は出ていて、「そのオンライン実験」を指していることになるため、読者はどのオンライン実験のことを指しているのかと疑問が湧き、混乱してしまうでしょう。

このように冠詞は文字数から見れば小さな存在ですが、文脈も変えてしまうほど、その役割はとても大きいのです。

Exercise　次の空所に適切な冠詞を入れましょう。

1. 森の中を歩いていて、落ちているりんごを 1 つ見つけたときの台詞
　　Oh, here is (　　　　　　　) apple.
2. 買って来たりんごをどこかに落としてしまい、それを見つけたときの台詞
　　Oh, here is (　　　　　　　) apple.

After You Read

DL 25　　CD2-21

A　会話を聞き、空所を埋めましょう。その後、会話をペアで練習しましょう。

Lily:　Aiden, are you ¹·_____ or something?

Aiden: Nope. This is Sans Forgetica, a new type of ²·_____ at RMIT University. This font is ³·_____ _____.

Lily:　Sounds interesting. I might want to use it for my next exam.

Aiden: You can visit their website ⁴·_____. It's free.

Lily:　But, it's not very easy to read a text written in this font.

Aiden: That is the very reason ⁵·_____ your memory.

Lily:　I see. That means, once you get used to this strangely shaped font, its magic power will disappear, doesn't it?

B　あなた自身の意見を考え、クラスメートと話し合いましょう。

1. How do you want to use Sans Forgetica?
2. Can you propose any other idea to boost your memory?

Behind the Scenes　望ましい困難

Sans Forgetica は「望ましい困難」(desirable difficulty) という認知心理学の原理に基づいて開発されたフォントです。「望ましい困難」は、カリフォルニア大学の心理学教授 Robert Allen Bjork が 1994 年に初めて提唱した概念で、彼は「困難」な課題は当初は学びの進みを遅くするが、長期的にみると学習の効果が大きく、さらに「望ましい」とはその課題が達成可能であることを意味する、と述べています。(参考:Desirable Difficulties Perspective on Learning—Bjork Learning and Forgetting Lab (pdf.))

Unit 13

How Fish Farms Can Use Facial Recognition to Survey Sick Salmon

顔認識されるのは、もう人間だけではありません。ノルウェーでサケの養殖を手がける Cermaq 社は顔認識ソフトを利用し、魚一匹ずつの健康状態を把握しようと計画しています。このシステムはサケの養殖業界に年間 10 億ドルもの損害をあたえているサケジラミの有効な駆除に役立つものと期待が寄せられています。

Before You Read

A 日本語の意味に合うように、空所に適切な語を語群から選んで書きましょう。語群には1つ余分なものがあります。

1. 顔認識ツールは犯罪捜査に用いられている
   facial recognition tools are used in criminal (　　　　　　)
2. 顔認識ソフトウエアを実装する　　　　(　　　　　　) the facial recognition software
3. 浮袋を調整する　　　　　　　　　(　　　　　　) their swim bladder
4. ピラミッド型の装置　　　　　　a pyramid-shaped (　　　　　)
5. サケジラミは魚の間に非常に偏って分布している
   sea lice are very (　　　　　) distributed amongst the fish

   | unevenly | device | investigations | implement | individually | regulate |

B 下線部の英語の意味として適切な日本語を空所に書きましょう。

1. <u>tag</u> your friends in photos on Facebook
   フェイスブックの写真で友人を（　　　　　　　）
2. use <u>face identification</u> technology in salmon farms
   サケの養殖場で（　　　　　　）技術を使う
3. <u>sort</u> salmon on the basis of weight　　重さを基にサケを（　　　　　　　）
4. <u>cut</u> fish mortality from sea lice
   サケジラミによる魚の死亡率を（　　　　　）
5. <u>bring down</u> the price of farmed salmon　　養殖サケの価格を（　　　　　）

Reading

1 Facial recognition tools are used in criminal investigations and when you tag your friends in photos on Facebook, but now, their usage is getting a little fishy—literally. A fish farm company hopes to use face
5 identification technology in high-tech salmon farms to check the animals for a parasite called sea lice and other health problems.

2 The Norwegian fish-farming firm Cermaq Group AS is planning on implementing the facial recognition software
10 as part of a high-tech fish farming suite they are calling iFarm, reports Agnieszka de Sousa at *Bloomberg Businessweek*. The tech, which should be ready for commercial use in five to six years, is likely going to be in high demand.

3 Currently, most fish farms assess the health of their
15 salmon as a group, not individually. If a few fish are found to have a disease or parasite, the whole farm is treated. But the iFarm system aims to assess each individual fish, allowing fish growers to determine how fast each fish grows and check for the presence of disease or parasites.

20 **4** To do this, the system will use a machine called the BioSort vision recognition system. De Sousa at *Bloomberg* reports that the system relies on the biology of the fish. In an iFarm, about 200,000 salmon would live in a 525-foot circular net. About every four days, salmon need to come
25 to the surface to take a gulp of air to regulate their swim bladder. When they do, a pyramid-shaped device guides them into the camera that recognizes their face based on the pattern of dots on their snout and gills and also scans their entire body. If the fish shows signs of a problem, it is
30 then guided into a holding pen for individual treatment.

5 "We know that sea lice are very unevenly distributed amongst the fish, and this system enables us to avoid mass lice treatments," Cermaq Norway Managing Director Knut

---

fishy 魚のような、怪しい

parasite 寄生生物
sea louse（複 lice）
サケジラミ

Cermaq Group AS
ノルウェーに本社をもつ世界有数のサーモン養殖企業

suite パッケージソフト

Bloomberg Businessweek
米国のブルームバーグより発行されているビジネス雑誌

grower 養殖者

vision recognition
視覚認識

gulp ゴクリと飲むこと
swim bladder （魚の）浮袋

snout 口先
gill （魚などの）えら

pen 囲い、いけす

amongst~ ～の間に
mass lice treatment
シラミの集団治療

Ellekjær tells Nicki Holmyard at *Seafood Source*. "Similarly,
35 we can sort salmon on the basis of weight and remove only
those fish ready for harvest, without stressing the others."

| 6   It's estimated that the system could cut fish mortality
from sea lice by 50 to 75 percent. Even when lice don't kill
the fish, the salmon are still rendered unsellable because of
40 the lesions and sores the lice cause.

| 7   "Only the fish that actually need it will be sorted out
for treatment, which means typically 5 to 20 percent," Geir
Stang Hauge, CEO of BioSort, the tech company collabo-
rating with Cermaq tells De Sousa. "This avoids stressful
45 treatment for all the healthy fish."

| 8   It's hoped that such a system would help bring down
the price of farmed salmon, which has become more expensive as the lice spread.

Notes

Seafood Source
海産物産業や専門家たちに業界
ニュースを初めとするさまざま
な情報を提供しているオンライ
ンサイト

mortality　死亡率

render *A B*
A を *B* の状態にする
unsellable　売れない
lesion　（皮膚の）損傷
sore　傷

BioSort
iFarm システムを開発したノル
ウェーの技術会社

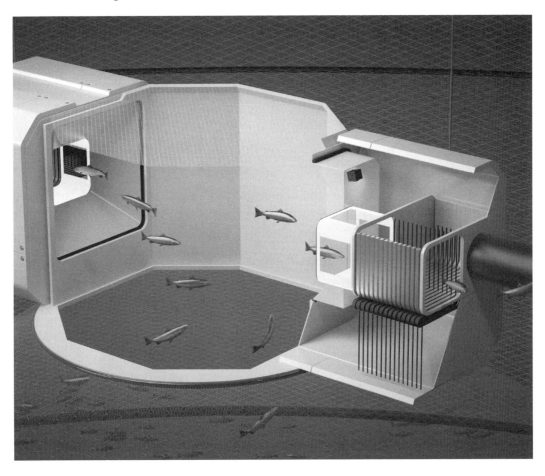

Comprehension Questions

A 記事の内容に一致するものには T（True）、一致しないものには F（False）を空所に書き入れましょう。

1. A fish farm company is planning to use face identification technology to examine the health conditions of the fish. ( )

2. The software, iFarm, has already been much in demand. ( )

3. At the moment, if there are any diseased fish in a farm, not only those fish but also the rest of the farm are treated. ( )

4. The point is that even though salmon do not breathe air, they need air to fill their swim bladder. ( )

5. Due to the uneven distribution of sea lice amongst the fish, the system cannot be fully effective. ( )

B 以下は記事の要約です。適切な語を空所に書き入れ、音声を聞いて答えを確認しましょう。 🎧 DL 26　◎ CD2-30

The Norwegian fish-farming firm Cermaq Group AS is planning to (¹· **i**　　　　) the iFarm system which allows them to assess the (²· **h**　　　　) of their salmon (³· **i**　　　　), thanks to facial recognition technology.

The iFarm will use a machine called the BioSort vision recognition system, which relies on the (⁴· **b**　　　　) of the fish. When salmon come to the surface to gulp air to (⁵· **r**　　　　) their swim bladder, a (⁶· **p**　　　) shaped device guides them into the camera that (⁷· **r**　　　　) their face and (⁸· **s**　　　) their entire body.

Since sea (⁹· **l**　　　　) are very (¹⁰· **u**　　　　) distributed amongst the fish, this system will avoid stressful treatment for all the healthy fish.

Read Better, Understand More!

接頭辞・接尾辞

一見知らない単語に思えても、接頭辞や接尾辞の役割が分かっていると意味が類推できることがあります。

例えば本文に出てきた grower は grow「育てる」＋ er（人を表す接尾辞）で、ここでは「養殖者」の意味です。

接尾辞の er は動詞に付いて、その動作をする人という意味の名詞を作ります。

例：advise「助言する」　→　adviser「助言者」
　　compose「作曲する」　→　composer「作曲家」

また unsellable も見慣れない単語かもしれませんが、un（否定を表す接頭辞）＋ sell「売る」＋ able（可能を表す接尾辞）の３つに分解できれば、「売れない」という意味の形容詞だと想像できるでしょう。

接頭辞の un は形容詞や名詞に付くと「不」「非」の意味を付け加え、動詞ではその動詞の行為が行われる前の状態に戻す、という意味に変えます。

例：willing「喜んでやる」　→　unwilling「気が進まない」
　　fasten「締める」　→　unfasten「外す、ほどく」

接尾辞の able は動詞に付いて、その行為が可能であるという形容詞を作ります。

例：bear「耐える」　→　bearable「耐えられる」
　　dispose「処分する」　→　disposable「使い捨ての」

このほか、理系の表現によく登場する接頭辞に anti がありますが、これは形容詞や名詞について「防止」「抗」などの意味を付け加えます。

例：aging「老化した」　→　antiaging「老化防止の」
　　body「体」　→　antibody「抗体」

Exercise　接頭辞や接尾辞をヒントに次の単語の意味を考えて書きましょう。

例：undo　　　　→　一旦したことを取り消す
1. goer　　　　→　（　　　　　　　　　）
2. antibacterial　→　（　　　　　　　　　）
3. admirable　　→　（　　　　　　　　　）

After You Read

会話を聞き、空所を埋めましょう。その後、会話をペアで練習しましょう。

🎧 DL 27　◎ CD2-31

Jacob: Mia, you know what? I went fishing yesterday and landed* a big salmon. This is the photo.

Mia: Gee, it's a huge salmon. But what is this 1.

_____ ?

Jacob: That is a sea louse, 2. _____

found on salmon. As sea lice cannot survive in fresh water, the presence suggests that this salmon must have returned to the river quite recently.

Mia: I see. Does that mean that the fish in the sea 3._____

_____ ?

Jacob: Yes, very much so. That's why a Norwegian fish-farming company plans to use a facial recognition system to 4._____

_____ of the fish by getting rid of the sea lice.

Mia: I thought a facial recognition system was only for humans.

Jacob: It may be 5._____ other than

fish.

*land：（魚を）釣り上げる

B あなた自身の意見を考え、クラスメートと話し合いましょう。

1. In your opinion, what will be the most difficult part of the facial-recognition system for salmon?

2. What are the other possible applications of the facial recognition tool?

Behind the Scenes　顔認識システム

顔認識システムは現在、さまざまな用途に使われています。日本入国管理局は 2017 年 10 月、東京国際空港（羽田）に顔認証ゲートを導入しました。これは、顔写真を撮影しパスポートと照合するもので、現在は成田、中部、関西および福岡空港でも利用されています。犯罪捜査に利用した例としては、2018 年 12 月 28 ～ 30 日に中国で開かれた香港の有名歌手のコンサート会場で監視カメラの顔認証システムを用いて逃亡中の容疑者 22 名を逮捕したことが報道されました（2019 年 1 月 1 日の毎日新聞）。一方、エンターテインメントの分野でもチケットの転売防止に顔認証が使われています。NEC の発表によれば、2014 年に「ももいろクローバー Z」が、NEC の顔認証システム「NeoFace」を導入したのが世界初の事例となりました。

14

Whales Change Their Tune Every Few Years

繁殖期のザトウクジラは歌を歌うシンガーです。この歌には流行があり、数年毎に新しいものが生まれてきます。一つの群れから別の群れへと歌が広がって行く様子は、まるで大洋規模で繰り広げられる伝言ゲームのようだ、と研究者は語ります。

Before You Read

A 日本語の意味に合うように、空所に適切な語を語群から選んで書きましょう。語群には１つ余分なものがあります。

1. オスは互いにメロディーを伝え合う　males (　　　　　　) tunes to one another
2. メスは歌わないようである　　　　females don't (　　　　) to sing
3. メロディーはますます複雑さを増すように進化していく
   the melodies (　　　　) to become increasingly complex
4. クジラたちはこのメロディーを捨て、新しい、より単純な歌を求める
   the whales (　　　　) the tune for a new and simpler song
5. 自らを目立たせるための飾り　　flourishes to (　　　　) themselves

   distinguish　transmit　drop　appear　evolve　sound

B 下線部の英語の意味として適切な日本語を空所に書きましょう。

1. the songs spread between populations
   これらの歌は (　　　　　　) 広がる
2. over the course of 13 consecutive years　13 年間 (　　　　　　)
3. put on an acoustic performance to attract females
   メスを引きつけるために (　　　　) パフォーマンスを披露する
4. abandon their sophisticated melody　　(　　　　　　) メロディーを捨てる
5. a limit to the whales' capacity to learn new material
   新しい曲を学ぶクジラの (　　　　　　) の限界

Reading

Notes

1 As they glide through the ocean, mighty humpback whales belt out complex melodies of moans, cries and squeaks. These sing-a-longs can last for hours, and males in a given population are known to transmit tunes to one
5　another; they add their own twists to the song, which are then picked up by other males. (Females don't appear to sing.) Gradually, the songs spread between populations, so that a tune from an Indian Ocean population, for instance, might crop up among humpbacks of the South Pacific—like
10　an ocean-wide game of telephone.

2 Now, as Roni Dengler reports for *Discover*, a new study has found that humpback whale songs don't stay the same forever. The melodies evolve to become increasingly complex over a period of a few years until, suddenly, the whales drop
15　the tune for a new and simpler song—something that the authors of the study, published in *Proceedings of the Royal Society B*, deem a "cultural revolution."

3 A team led by marine biologist Jenny Allen of the University of Queensland analyzed recordings of eastern
20　Australian humpback whales, taken over the course of 13 consecutive years. In total, according to Virginia Morell of *Science*, they looked at 412 song cycles from 95 singers, scoring the ditties' complexity based on the number of sounds, themes and variations.

25　**4** The researchers found that the songs gradually evolve to become longer and include more parts, possibly due to flourishes that individual males come up with to distinguish themselves from the rest of the chorus. Scientists don't know precisely why male humpbacks sing, but some
30　have theorized that they are putting on an acoustic performance to attract females—or even to impress their male buddies.

5 "Since all the males in a population sing the same

glide　静かに滑るように動く
mighty　巨大な
humpback whale
ザトウクジラ
belt out ～
（歌を）大きな声で歌う
moan　うめき
squeak　キーキー声
twist　新しい工夫

crop up　現れる

game of telephone
伝言ゲーム
Discover
ディスカバー誌（米国のサイエンス誌）

Proceedings of the Royal Society B
英国王立協会紀要 B（生物学関連の文献集）
deem　考える

University of Queensland
クイーンズランド大学
over the course of ～
～にわたって

Science
サイエンス誌。アメリカ科学振興協会によって発行されている学術雑誌。
ditty　（短い）歌
theme　主題
variation　変奏

flourish　装飾
come up with ～
～を考え出す
chorus　群れ

theorize　理論化する
put on ～　～を披露する

buddy　仲間

song, small changes might be an opportunity to stand out
35 from the crowd," Allen tells Dengler.

| 6 Every few years, however, the whales abandon their
sophisticated melody in favor of a sparser song. The researchers aren't sure why, but paring down the tune might
give humpbacks a new opportunity to add their own embel-
40 lishments. In a University of Queensland video, Allen com-
pares the whales' shifting song preferences to the ebb and
flow of fashion trends among humans.

| 7 "When a new fashion trend comes in, everybody wants
to look new and slightly different," she says, "so everybody
45 will incorporate that fashion trend until it becomes the
norm."

| 8 It is also possible that, after a certain point, the whales
just can't keep up with the increasingly elaborate songs.
There may be "a limit to the whales' capacity to learn new
50 material," Allen explains.

| 9 But make no mistake: humpback whales are highly
sophisticated creatures. Their ability to transmit songs,
not just within populations, but also between them, "is cultural transmission on a scale comparable to what we find
55 in people," according to Allen. Having a better understanding of what drives cultural and social learning in whales
could, therefore, help scientists gain new insight into why
these traits have evolved with unparalleled complexity in
humans.

Notes

sparse　まばらな、希薄な

pare down ~
～をシンプルにする
embellishment　装飾

ebb and flow　盛衰

unparalleled　前代未聞の

Comprehension Questions

A 記事の内容に一致するものには T（True）、一致しないものには F（False）を空所に書き入れましょう。

1. Humpback whales moan, cry and sing loudly complex melodies together as they swim.　　　　　　（　　　）

2. The males in a given population add small changes to the song, and then other males pick up the changes.　　　　　　（　　　）

3. The melodies develop to become more sophisticated for a few years, then the whales suddenly start to sing a new song which is much simpler than the old one.　　　　　　（　　　）

4. Marine biologists studied 412 song cycles from 95 singers including both male and female whales, and scored the songs' complexity.　　　　　　（　　　）

5. The reason why the songs gradually evolve to become longer and more complex can be that individual males add flourishes to distinguish themselves from the rest of the group.　　　　　　（　　　）

B 以下は記事の要約です。適切な語を空所に書き入れ、音声を聞いて答えを確認しましょう。　　　🎧 DL 28　　⊚ CD2-41

　Humpback whales are known to sing a song in water for hours. The (¹· t　　　　　　) are (²· t　　　　　　) not only within a population but also between different populations.

　Scientists don't know (³· p　　　　　　) why male humpbacks sing, but some have (⁴· t　　　　　) that they are performing acoustically to (⁵· a　　　　) females—or even to (⁶· i　　　　) their male buddies.

　Now, a new study has revealed that humpback whale songs don't (⁷· s　　　　) the same forever. (⁸· E　　　　　) few years, the song is replaced with a new and (⁹· s　　　　) one. Two possible (¹⁰· i　　　　): this may give them a new opportunity to add their own modifications, or there may be "a limit to the whales' (¹¹· c　　　　) to learn new material."

Read Better, Understand More!

接尾辞「ly」

形容詞（形容詞の働きをする動詞の現在分詞も含む）に接尾辞 ly がつくと副詞になります。本文でも多数登場しています。

gradually	徐々に	(gradual（形容詞）+ ly)
increasingly	ますます	(increasing（動詞の現在分詞）+ ly)
suddenly	突然に	(sudden（形容詞）+ ly)
possibly	おそらく	(possible（形容詞）+ ly)
precisely	正確に	(precise（形容詞）+ ly)
slightly	わずかに	(slight（形容詞）+ ly)
highly	高く、高度に	(high（形容詞）+ ly)

接尾語の ly には「〜のような」「〜らしい」という意味をもつものもあり、これが形容詞の後につくと副詞にはならず、形容詞のままで意味を変えます。例えば、elderly「年配の」は elder「年上の」という形容詞から生まれた形容詞です。

さらに ly には「〜にふさわしい」という意味もあり、これが名詞の後につくと、名詞は形容詞になります。例えば、time「時間」に ly がついた timely は「時機を得た」という意味の形容詞、friend「友人」に ly がついた friendly は「友好的な」という意味の形容詞、day「日」に ly がついた daily は「毎日の、日刊の」という意味の形容詞です。

Exercise 次の単語に ly がついた単語の品詞と意味を書きましょう。

例：final［形容詞］　　→　finally　品詞：［副詞］意味：（最終的に）

1. intentional［形容詞］
   →　intentionally　品詞：［　　　　　　　　］意味：（　　　　　　　　）
2. man［名詞］
   →　manly　品詞：［　　　　　　　　］意味：（　　　　　　　　）
3. good［形容詞］
   →　goodly　品詞：［　　　　　　　　］意味：（　　　　　　　　）

After You Read

A 会話を聞き、空所を埋めましょう。その後、会話をペアで練習しましょう。

🎧 DL 29　　⊙ CD2-42

Mark: Lisa, did you know that ¹· _____?

Lisa: Yes, it's ²· _____, right? In water, light cannot reach far, but sound can travel a long distance at a high speed.

Mark: Well, scientists don't know exactly why they sing, but they found that males in one population ³· _____.

Lisa: You mean they sing the same song?

Mark: Yes, and the songs ⁴· _____ since each whale adds something new to the song.

Lisa: That's interesting. I wonder if they want ⁵· _____

_____.

Mark: That's possible. Whales cannot change their hair color or wear bizarre* costumes, after all.

*bizarre：奇妙な、風変わりな

B あなた自身の意見を考え、クラスメートと話し合いましょう。

1. Do you agree with the theory of some researchers that humpback whales sing songs to attract females?
2. What are other tactics for animals to attract females?

Behind the Scenes　　クジラの歌

歌を歌うクジラとして、ザトウクジラ以外にもシロナガスクジラ（blue whale）やナガスクジラ（fin whale）の研究が報告されています。米国地球物理学連合の 2018 年 11 月 28 日付けの記事によれば、シロナガスクジラやナガスクジラは海洋生物中で体も声も最大級の大きさをもち、オスの歌う歌は大型船舶の発する汽笛並の大きさで、海中を 1000 キロメートル以上も伝わり、大洋の中でクジラ同士が交信するのに役立っているとのことです。

Your Christmas Tree May Be Turned Into Mouthwash One Day

クリスマスが終わると、道ばたに捨てられ回収車に積み込まれるのを待つモミの木たち。これまでは埋め立てゴミとして処分される運命だった使用済みのクリスマスツリーの新しい利用法の研究が始まっています。いつの日かツリーはマウスウォッシュに生まれ変わるかもしれません。

Before You Read

A 日本語の意味に合うように、空所に適切な語を語群から選んで書きましょう。語群には１つ余分なものがあります。

1. これらの常緑樹は廃棄される　　　　　these evergreens are (　　　　　　　)
2. 温室効果ガスを放出する　　　　　　(　　　　　　　) greenhouse gases
3. バイオリファイナリーは未開のプロセスを用いることができるだろう
   biorefineries would be able to use an (　　　　　　) process
4. グリセロールのような溶媒　　　　　(　　　　　　　) like glycerol
5. マツに存在するピネンを環境にやさしいプラスチックへ変換する
   (　　　　　　) pinene found in pine trees into a sustainable plastic

> **abandoned　feedstocks　unexplored　solvents　emit　convert**

B 下線部の英語の意味として適切な日本語を空所に書きましょう。

1. your Christmas tree may be <u>turned into</u> mouthwash
   あなたのクリスマスツリーがマウスウォッシュ (　　　　　　　) かもしれない
2. they <u>are composed of</u> a complex polymer
   それらは複雑なポリマー (　　　　　　　)
3. <u>be refined</u> into glucose　　　　グルコースへと (　　　　　　)
4. <u>utilize</u> the trees　　　　これらの木を (　　　　　　)
5. mouthwash and paint are not the only things pine needles <u>are good for</u>
   松葉が (　　　　　　) のはマウスウォッシュや塗料だけではない

Reading

CD2-43 ～ CD2-49

Notes

1 'Tis the season … to kick millions of Christmas trees to the curb.

2 In some places they've gotten creative with these abandoned evergreens, turning them into mulch, using
5 them as erosion barriers or sinking them in lakes to create fish habitat. But in many places the trees are simply tossed in the landfill, where their pine needles break down, emitting greenhouse gases. Now, researchers at the University of Sheffield are offering a sustainable alternative to this
10 sad fate.

3 The problem with pine needles is that they are mostly composed of a complex polymer known as lignocellulose, whose chemical structure makes it unsuitable for biomass energy, in which wood, grass and paper and other organic
15 materials are broken down into ethanol. However, as Mark Kinver at the *BBC* reports, Cynthia Kartey, a chemical engineer, found another use for pine needles. As it turns out, they are a great feedstock for creating other chemicals.

4 "My research has been focused on the breakdown of
20 this complex structure into simple, high-valued industrial chemical feedstocks such as sugars and phenolics, which are used in products like household cleaners and mouthwash," says Kartey, a doctoral candidate at Sheffield, in a press release. "Biorefineries would be able to use a relative-
25 ly simple but unexplored process to break down the pine needles."

5 Using heat and solvents like cheap, environmentally friendly glycerol, the needles can be broken down into bio-oil and bio-char. Bio-oil can be further refined into glu-
30 cose, which is used as a food sweetener, acetic acid used in making paint and adhesives, and phenol, which is used in mouthwash. The solid bio-char also has industrial uses. "In the future, the tree that decorated your house over the

'tis it is の短縮形（詩などで使われる）
curb 歩道の縁石

evergreen 常緑樹
mulch 根覆い
erosion 浸食

habitat 生息場所

landfill ごみ埋め立て地

University of Sheffield シェフィールド大学

polymer ポリマー、重合体
lignocellulose リグノセルロース

ethanol エタノール

BBC 英国放送協会

feedstock 原料

phenolics フェノール類

doctoral candidate 博士号取得候補者

glycerol グリセロール
bio-oil バイオオイル
bio-char バイオ炭
glucose ブドウ糖
acetic acid 酢酸

adhesive 接着剤
phenol フェノール

92

festive period could be turned into paint to decorate your
35 house once again," Kartey says.

|6| The *BBC* reports that in the UK, about 8 million real
Christmas trees are purchased each year. Seven million
of those trees end up in landfills. Utilizing the trees as a
chemical feedstock, instead, would reduce the country's
40 carbon footprint and help replace toxic chemicals with less
harmful ones. That's something the US should take note of,
considering 25 to 30 million real Christmas trees are put
up each year here.

|7| Mouthwash and paint are not the only things pine
45 needles are good for. Earlier this year, chemists at the
University of Bath found that they could convert an organic
compound found in pine trees called pinene (aptly named,
as it's responsible for producing that distinct scent), into
a type of sustainable plastic through a four-step process,
50 reports Alyssa Danigelis at *Seeker*.

Notes

festive 祝祭の

carbon footprint
二酸化炭素排出量

University of Bath
バース大学
pinene ピネン
aptly 適切に、うまく

Seeker
米国のテック・サイエンス系メ
ディア

Extra Notes

biomass：バイオ（bio＝生物）とマス（mass＝量）を組み合わせた言葉。化石燃料を除く、植物などの生物から生まれた再生できる資源のこと。　**biorefinery**：生物精製所。再生可能な資源であるバイオマスからバイオエネルギー、バイオ燃料や有用な化合物などを製造するプラント。

Comprehension Questions

A 記事の内容に一致するものには T（True）、一致しないものには F（False）を空所に書き入れましょう。

1. Pine needles are not suitable for biomass energy production because of their main component, lignocellulose. (　　)

2. A doctoral candidate at University of Sheffield found a simple way to break down the complex structure into ethanol. (　　)

3. When tossed in a landfill, Christmas trees emit greenhouse gasses, but when utilized as a chemical feedstock, the sum of produced greenhouse gasses would be reduced. (　　)

4. British people purchase about 8 million real Christmas trees every year, and 7 million of those trees are wasted in landfills, leaving only less than 1 million for reutilization. (　　)

5. Scientists at University of Bath gave up an idea to convert pinene into a type of sustainable plastic. (　　)

B 以下は記事の要約です。適切な語を空所に書き入れ、音声を聞いて答えを確認しましょう。　　🎧 DL 30　　💿 CD2-50

Every year millions of real Christmas trees are (1. **p**　　　　　) in the UK, but most of them end up in landfills, where the pine needles (2. **b**　　　　) down, emitting carbon dioxide and other (3. **g**　　　　　) gases. Pine needles composed of a complex (4. **p**　　　　), lignocellulose, are not suitable for (5. **b**　　　　　) energy in contrast to other organic materials which are broken down into ethanol. Now a chemical engineer has found a way to (6. **c**　　　　) the needles into bio-oil and bio-char by using heat and solvents like cheap, (7. **e**　　　　) friendly glycerol. This bio-oil can be further (8. **r**　　　　) into (9. **g**　　　　　), acetic acid and (10. **p**　　　　), which is used in mouthwash. Utilizing the trees as a chemical (11. **f**　　　　) would reduce not only the carbon footprint but also the consumption of toxic chemicals.

Read Better, Understand More!

物質名詞が普通名詞になるとき

日常的には物質名詞であるものが、科学の文脈では普通名詞になる場合がしばしばあります。例えば、本文にも登場した sugar は日常的には「砂糖」の意味で使われ、不定冠詞の a がついたり、複数形 sugars になったりしない物質名詞です。ところが、本文では下記のように複数形で使用されていました。

"My research has been focused on the breakdown of this complex structure into simple, high-valued industrial chemical feedstocks such as <u>sugars</u> and phenolics ..."

その理由は、ここでは sugars が「砂糖」を意味するのではなく、グルコースを初めとするさまざまな糖を意味しているからなのです。

ちなみに通常「砂糖」と呼んでいるこの物質の正しい化学名は「ショ糖」で、英語名は sucrose です。そして sucrose という物質は一種類しかないため、a がついたり、複数形になったりしません。一方 sugar「糖」にはさまざまな種類（例えば、グルコースやフルクトースなどの単糖、スクロースなどの二糖、オリゴ糖や多糖など）が存在するために、1つ、2つと数え上げることができる普通名詞になるのです。

他にも例を挙げてみましょう。salt「塩」（正しい化学名は「塩化ナトリウム」で英語名は sodium chloride）は日常で用いられるとき a がついたり、複数形になったりしない物質名詞ですが、科学の文脈で使われるとき、salt は酸と塩基が反応して生じる「塩」を意味し、普通名詞になります。

例：An acid reacts with a base to form a salt.「酸と塩基が反応して塩が生じる」

Exercise 日本語と同じ意味になるように、空所に必要な冠詞を書きましょう。冠詞が必要ないときには×を書きましょう。

1. 私はアルコールに弱い。　　　I am weak to (　　　　　　) alcohol.

2. 化学ではアルコールとはヒドロキシ基が炭素原子に結合している有機化合物のことである。

In chemistry, (　　　　　　) alcohol is any organic compound in which a hydroxy functional group (-OH) is bound to a carbon atom.

3. 塩は陽イオンと陰イオンからなる。

(　　　　　　) salt consists of (　　　　　　) cation and (　　　　　　) anion.

After You Read

DL 31　CD2-51

A 会話を聞き、空所を埋めましょう。その後、会話をペアで練習しましょう。

Ryan: Ellie, do you know what ¹· _____
after Christmas?

Ellie: Let me see … I think some trees are recycled, but most of them are ²· _____
_____ .

Ryan: Today, I read an interesting article ³· _____
_____ . Our Christmas tree may be turned into mouthwash one day!

Ellie: I can't find any connection between Christmas trees and mouthwash.

Ryan: Well, researchers are trying to break them down into ⁴· _____
_____ such as glucose, acetic acid and phenol, which
is used in mouthwash.

Ellie: Science is advancing every day! But, come to think of it, we don't have to
use real trees for Christmas; there are ⁵· _____
_____ .

Ryan: I totally agree with you. Felling* the trees every year and using them only
for a few weeks is a waste of natural resources.

*fell：伐採する

B あなた自身の意見を考え、クラスメートと話し合いましょう。

1. Do you recycle anything? Or, do you separate specific materials, such as plastic
bottles, metal cans, paper and glass, from garbage?
2. Do you want to put up a real Christmas tree for Christmas? Why or why not?

Behind the Scenes　バイオマスとバイオリファイナリー

バイオリファイナリー（生物精製所）は、再生可能な資源であるバイオマスからバイオ
エネルギー、バイオ燃料を始めとする有用な化合物を製造するプラントで、石油を精製
するオイルリファイナリー（石油精製所）に比べ、数々の利点をもっています。石油と
いう限りある資源ではなくバイオマスという再生可能な資源を使用すること、地球温暖
化防止につながるなど環境負荷が小さいことです。

Acknowledgements

All the materials are reprinted by permission of the copyright holders.

Text Credits

Unit 1 Flowers Sweeten Up When They Sense Bees Buzzing

Flowers Sweeten Up When They Sense Bees Buzzing
https://www.smithsonianmag.com/smart-news/flowers-sweeten-when-they-hear-bees-buzzing-180971300/

Unit 2 Sorry, the Mona Lisa Is Not Looking at You

Sorry, the Mona Lisa Is Not Looking at You
https://www.smithsonianmag.com/smart-news/sorry-mona-lisa-not-looking-you-180971207/

Unit 3 Nearly One-Third of Americans Sleep Fewer Than Six Hours Per Night

Nearly One-Third of Americans Sleep Fewer Than Six Hours Per Night
https://www.smithsonianmag.com/smart-news/almost-one-third-americans-sleep-fewer-six-hours-night-180971116/

Unit 4 There's No Limit on Longevity, But Getting Super Old Is Still Tough

Study Suggests There's No Limit on Longevity, But Getting Super Old Is Still Tough
https://www.smithsonianmag.com/smart-news/study-suggests-theres-no-limit-longevity-getting-super-old-still-tough-180969488/

Unit 5 Chinese City Wants to Launch Fake Moon to Illuminate Its Streets

Chinese City Wants to Launch Fake Moon to Illuminate Its Streets
https://www.smithsonianmag.com/smart-news/chinese-city-wants-launch-fake-moon-illuminate-its-streets-180970576/

Unit 6 Doctors "Grow" Ear for Transplant in Patient's Forearm

Doctors 'Grow' Ear for Transplant in Patient's Forearm
https://www.smithsonianmag.com/smart-news/doctors-grew-ear-soldiers-forearm-then-used-it-ear-transplant-180969058/

Unit 7 A German Grocery Chain Is Selling First-Of-Its-Kind "No-Kill" Eggs

A German Grocery Chain Is Selling First-Of-Its-Kind "No-Kill" Eggs
https://www.smithsonianmag.com/smart-news/what-no-kill-eggs-are-now-available-berlin-supermarkets-180971117/

Unit 8 Why Scientists Want to Engineer Spicy Tomatoes

Why Scientists Want to Engineer Spicy Tomatoes
https://www.smithsonianmag.com/smart-news/why-scientists-want-engineer-spicy-tomatoes-180971201/

Unit 9 Children Are Susceptible to Robot Peer Pressure

Children Are Susceptible to Robot Peer Pressure, Study Suggests
https://www.smithsonianmag.com/smart-news/children-are-susceptible-robot-peer-pressure-study-suggests-180970047/#zkyMePlCmdDlPCfZ.99

Unit 10 British Doctors May Soon Prescribe Art, Music, Dance, Singing Lessons

British Doctors May Soon Prescribe Art, Music, Dance, Singing Lessons
https://www.smithsonianmag.com/smart-news/british-doctors-may-soon-prescribe-art-music-dance-singing-lessons-180970750/

Unit 11 This Remote Control Vest Trains Rescue Dogs Using Flashlights

This Remote Control Vest Trains Rescue Dogs Using Flashlights https://www.smithsonianmag.com/smart-news/vest-makes-search-and-rescue-dogs-remote-control-180970734/

References:
H. Nishinoma et al., "Canine Motion Control using Bright Spotlight Devices Mounted on a Suit," in IEEE Transactions on Medical Robotics and Bionics.
doi: 10.1109/TMRB.2019.2930343
keywords: {Laser beams;Dogs;Brightness;Radiation effects;Light emitting diodes;Lenses;Animals;Biological Control Systems;Navigation;Optics.},
http://ieeexplore.ieee.org/stamp/stamp.jsp?tp=&arnumber=8770263&isnumber=8627956

Kazunori Ohno, Ryunosuke Hamada, Tatsuya Hoshi, Hiroyuki Nishinoma, Shumpei Yamaguchi, Solvi Arnold, Kimitoshi Yamazaki, Takafumi Kikusui, Satoko Matsubara, Mihi Nagasawa, Takatomi Kubo, Eri Nakahara, Yuki Maruno, Kazushi Ikeda, Toshitaka Yamakawa, Takeshi Tokuyama, Ayumi Shinohara, Ryo Yoshinaka, Diptarama Hendrian, Kaizaburo Chubachi, Satoshi Kobayashi, Katsuhito Nakashima, Hiroaki Naganuma, Ryu Wakimoto, Shu Ishikawa, Tatsuki Miura and Satoshi Tadokoro, Cyber-Enhanced Rescue Canine, Disaster Robotics - Results from the ImPACT Tough Robotics Challenge, Satoshi Tadokoro Ed., Springer Tracts in Advanced Robotics 128, pp. 143-193, DOI: 10.1007/978-3-030-05321-5_4, 2019.

Unit 12 Sans Forgetica Is the Typeface You Won't Forget
Sans Forgetica is the Typeface You Won't Forget
https://www.smithsonianmag.com/smart-news/sans-forgetica-trippy-new-typeface-could-help-readers-remember-what-they-read-180970485/

Unit 13 How Fish Farms Can Use Facial Recognition to Survey Sick Salmon
How Fish Farms Can Use Facial Recognition to Survey Sick Salmon
https://www.smithsonianmag.com/smart-news/facial-recognition-will-be-used-monitor-fish-faces-180970493/

Unit 14 Whales Change Their Tune Every Few Years
Whales Change Their Tune Every Few Years
https://www.smithsonianmag.com/smart-news/whale-songs-undergo-cultural-revolutions-180970880/

Unit 15 Your Christmas Tree May Be Turned Into Mouthwash One Day
Your Christmas Tree May Be Turned Into Mouthwash One Day
https://www.smithsonianmag.com/smart-news/one-day-your-christmas-tree-may-be-turned-mouthwash-180971133/#Ck7coCrovqwQjx8K.99

Photo Credits
Unit 2
Amira Aziz | Dreamstime.com
Shuo Wang | Dreamstime.com

Unit 9
University of Plymouth

Unit 11
Kazunori Ohno, NICHe, Tohoku University, Japan

Unit 12
RMIT University

Unit 13
Cermaq

本書には音声CD（別売）があります

Science at Hand
Articles from Smithsonian Magazine's Smart News
スミソニアンで読む日常の科学

2020年1月20日　初版第1刷発行
2023年2月20日　初版第8刷発行

編著者　　宮本　惠子

発行者　　福岡　正人

発行所　　株式会社　金星堂

〒101-0051　東京都千代田区神田神保町 3-21
Tel.　(03) 3263-3828（営業部）
　　　(03) 3263-3997（編集部）
Fax　(03) 3263-0716
http://www.kinsei-do.co.jp

編集担当　池田恭子　　　　　　　　　　Printed in Japan
印刷所／日新印刷株式会社　製本所／松島製本
本書の無断複製・複写は著作権法上での例外を除き禁じられています。
本書を代行業者等の第三者に依頼してスキャンやデジタル化することは、
たとえ個人や家庭内での利用であっても認められておりません。
落丁・乱丁本はお取り替えいたします。
ISBN978-4-7647-4103-4　　C1082